WRITERS AND THEIR WORK

ISOBEL ARMSTRONG
General Editor

T0341699

D. M. THOMAS

D. M. THOMAS

D. M. THOMAS

Bran Nicol

Northcote House
in association with the
British Council

For Karen and Joe

© Copyright 2004 by Bran Nicol

First published in 2004 by Northcote House Publishers Ltd, Horndon, Tavistock, Devon, PL19 9NQ, United Kingdom.
Tel: +44 (01822) 810066. Fax: +44 (01822) 810034.

British Library Cataloguing-in-Publication Data
A catalogue record for this book is available from the British Library

ISBN 0-7463-1123-0 hardback
ISBN 0-7463-0942-2 paperback

Typeset by TW Typesetting, Plymouth, Devon
Printed and bound by CPI Group (UK) Ltd, Croydon, CR0 4YY

Contents

Acknowledgements

I would like to express my thanks to: Jan Ainsley for her kindness, Joanna Jellinek for her thoughtful editorship, Ben Noys for his wisdom, Niki Murray for her enthusiasm, James Simpson for his library and, most of all, Karen Stevens and Joe Furness, for their love and laughter.

Biographical Outline

1935   Donald Michael Thomas born in Redruth, Cornwall, to parents Harold and Amy Thomas. Educated at Redruth Grammar School.

1949   The family emigrates to Australia, following sister Lois's marriage to an Australian soldier. Thomas begins to go through puberty on long voyage, an experience he will never forget and will return to often in his work. He attends University High School, Melbourne.

1951   The family returns to England, where Thomas begins National Service, spending most of it learning Russian. He is graded 'suitable for low-level interrogation' in Russian.

1955   Reads English, New College Oxford. Publishes a short story, 'The Opportunist' in Oxford University magazine *Isis* under the name Donald Thomas.

1958   Graduates with First Class degree, taking MA. Takes Diploma of Education at Oxford, during which time he begins writing poetry.

1959   Takes up post as English teacher at Teignmouth Grammar School.

1960   Death of Harold Thomas.

1963   Becomes lecturer in English, Hereford College of Education, eventually becoming Head of Department.

1964   First pamphlet of poems, *Personal and Possessive*, is published.

1967   Takes up Fellowship in Writing, University of Minnesota, St Paul, Minnesota.

1968	*Penguin Modern Poets 11* (along with Peter Redgrove and D. M. Black). *Two Voices* (poetry).
1971	*Logan Stone* (poetry).
1973	*The Shaft* (poetry).
1975	Death of Amy Thomas. *Love and Other Deaths* (poetry).
1976	*Requiem* and *Poem Without a Hero* (translations of Akhmatova).
1977	*The Honeymoon Voyage* (poetry). Hereford College closed down; returns to Oxford for BLitt, 'Problems in Translating Pushkin', which he never finishes.
1978	*Dreaming in Bronze* (poetry; winner of Cholmondeley Award).
1979	*Way of All the Earth* (translation of the poems of Anna Akhmatova); *The Flute-Player* wins Gollancz/Picador/Guardian Fantasy Prize.
1980	*Birthstone*, Thomas's first novel, originally begun in collaboration with Elizabeth Ashworth.
1981	*The White Hotel* (novel) published to mixed reviews in England. Nominated for Booker Prize.
1982	Thomas's 'annus mirabilis': after enthusiastic reviews in the United States *The White Hotel* becomes international bestseller (winning PEN Prize, *Los Angeles Times* Fiction Prize, and the Cheltenham Prize). January: takes up five-month post as Lecturer in Creative Writing, American University in Washington, and controversially leaves post one week later. Letter to the *Times Literary Supplement* charging Thomas of plagiarism in *The White Hotel* sparks off six-week debate, and is followed by further allegations. *You Will Hear Thunder* (Akhmatova, radio play)
1983	*Ararat*, first in *Russian Nights* sequence of novels.
1984	Play version of *The White Hotel*, adapted by Thomas, performed at Edinburgh Festival; *Boris Godunov* (adaptation of Pushkin's play for radio). *Swallow* (*Russian Nights*, 2).
1986	*Sphinx* (*Russian Nights*, 3)

1987	Returns to live in Truro. *Summit* (*Russian Nights*, 4). Thomas suffers nervous breakdown and enters psychoanalysis for the first time.
1988	Publishes memoir, *Memories and Hallucinations*.
1990	*Lying Together* brings *Russian Nights* quintet to a close.
1992	*Flying in to Love* (novel).
1993	*Pictures at an Exhibition*, Thomas's second novel to blend psychoanalysis and the holocaust is published, raising Thomas's profile again amidst accusations of exploiting sensitive subject matter.
1994	*Eating Pavlova* (novel).
1998	Publication of *Alexander Solzhenitsyn*, a biography four years in the writing. *Lady with a Laptop* (novel, only appears in the United States).
2000	*Charlotte* (novel).

Abbreviations and References

Unless otherwise stated, all books and articles listed below are by D. M. Thomas.

A   *Ararat*, 1983 (London: Sphere Books, 1984)

AE   'Altering My Ego', *Guardian*, 3 March 1993, 4, 6

B   *Birthstone*, 1980 (Harmondsworth: Penguin, 1982)

C   *Charlotte* (London: Duckworth, 2000)

DW   David Wingrove, interview with D. M. Thomas, *London Magazine*, February 1982, 27–43

EP   *Eating Pavlova*, 1994 (London: Sceptre, 1995)

FL   *Flying in to Love*, 1992 (London: Sceptre, 1993)

FP   *The Flute-Player*, 1979 (London: Picador, 1982)

LC   'On Literary Celebrity', *New York Times Magazine* 13 June 1982, 24–9; available on <http://www.nytimes.com/books>

LT   *Lying Together*, 1990 (London: Sphere Books, 1991)

MH   *Memories and Hallucinations* (London: Victor Gollancz, 1988)

PE   *Pictures at an Exhibition*, 1993 (London: Sceptre, 1994)

Sw   *Swallow*, 1984 (London: Sphere Books, 1987)

Sph   *Sphinx*, 1986 (London: Sphere Books, 1987)

Sum   *Summit*, 1987 (London: Sphere Books, 1988)

SL   Stephen Lewis, interview with D. M. Thomas in *Art out of Agony: The Holocaust Theme in Literature, Sculpture and Film* (Toronto, Canada: Canadian Broadcasting Corporation, 1984), 71–88

WH   *The White Hotel*, 1981 (London: Indigo, 1996)

1

Introduction: Doubting Thomas

Novelist, poet, translator. Opportunist, plagiarist, pornographer. D. M. Thomas has had many identities throughout his career. Critical opinion about his work has tended to be sharply divided between those who laud his writing as powerful and innovative, and those who find something reprehensible about the books and the author who wrote them. My opinion, naturally, is that Thomas is one of the most important writers of our time, and this book will mostly be about why. Yet any consideration of his work must take into account the controversy which has surrounded it, partly because it has been so continuous, but mainly because Thomas's capacity to provoke is intimately bound up with the most distinctive feature of his work: its obsession with exploring, and enacting, the blurring of boundaries.

Thomas is best known as the author of *The White Hotel* (1981), his novel about one woman's confrontation with two of the most powerful and representative ideologies of the twentieth century: Lisa Erdman's hysterical symptoms are treated by Sigmund Freud, the founder of psychoanalysis, only for it to transpire that her condition is not the result of past trauma but an apprehension of her own violent death in the Nazi death camps. *The White Hotel* is compelling and beautifully written and one of the most remarkable novels of the second half of the twentieth century. It brings together so powerfully the enduring obsessions of an obsessive writer that it seems all Thomas's work leading up to it is in some ways a rehearsal and all the work that follows a reprise. Yet this only partly

1

explains the curious fact that it is the only one of Thomas's works to have been the subject of any sustained discussion by academics, though he has also written eleven other novels, numerous volumes of poetry and acclaimed translations of Russian poetry.

The White Hotel owed its initial success to the peculiar appeal it seemed to hold for the American consciousness – perhaps because, as Martin Amis said, it deals with the three 'national fixations', sex, the Final Solution and psychoanalysis.[1] Enthusiastic reviews in the United States turned it into an instant 'contemporary classic' and its initial English sales of around 700 copies were dwarfed by a US paperback print run of a million copies. It became the subject of the kind of 'hype' more often employed in the marketing of films, where what is sold is not just the product itself but the 'concept' of the product. The book appeared with five different covers, and key rings and T-shirts were made to promote it. Thomas himself naturally became caught up in the hype too. Without warning, an obscure English poet and former schoolmaster (as the American press liked to characterize him) found himself catapulted into a world of TV appearances and tabloid prurience quite unlike the pattern of reading tours and newspaper interviews normally afforded major authors. The result was that in January 1982 Thomas abruptly quit a semester-long post teaching creative writing at the American University in Washington almost as soon as it had begun. As he explained in his hasty letter of resignation, he was worried that his celebrity was transforming him from a teacher of creative writing into a 'media monster'.[2] His departure in fact made this a self-fulfilling prophecy. It was obviously newsworthy, particularly as its 'here today gone tomorrow' quality aptly echoed the idea of overnight success. Rather than diminishing his fame, 'The Flight of D. M. Thomas', as one newspaper dubbed it, only increased it.

No sooner had this 'scandal' died down than another, more serious, controversy developed around *The White Hotel*. Following the American response, the novel became a bestseller in England, too, and just missed out on winning the 1981 Booker Prize. In March 1982 a letter appeared in the *Times Literary Supplement* alleging that Thomas had plagiarised *Babi*

2

Yar (1970) by Russian novelist Anatoli Kuznetsov.[3] Kuznetsov's book contains a transcript of one of the few eye-witness accounts of the massacre, by a Ukrainian woman Dina Pronicheva, and Thomas incorporates this testimony into his own heroine's story in the penultimate chapter of *The White Hotel*, with only minor adjustments. Though Thomas provided an acknowledgement of his use of Kuznetsov on the copyright page, this small-print reference was considered by some to be at odds with the extensive, often word for word, borrowings from the novel.

The *TLS* debate rumbled on for a total of six weeks, and included further hostile letters as well as Thomas's own eloquent defence and a symposium on plagiarism featuring distinguished voices like Ian McEwan and Harold Bloom.[4] Once the spotlight of plagiarism was turned on Thomas, other suspicions were raised. One contributor to the *TLS* debate, the critic Geoffrey Grigson, wondered about an early group of Thomas's poems which, by the author's own admission, had 'evolved from myths suggested by science-fiction stories' by a number of writers.[5] Then in September and November 1982 two further plagiarism controversies blew up surrounding Thomas's translations of the Russian poets Pushkin (in *The Bronze Horseman*, 1982) and Akhmatova (*Requiem and Poem Without a Hero*, 1976). In both cases American professors of Russian literature argued that Thomas's translations depended too heavily on previous versions by other translators, repeating unintentionally the mistakes and peculiarities of their work. In 1983 Thomas was accused by the historian Christopher Walker of using unacknowledged statistics about the 1915 Armenian holocaust in his 1983 novel *Ararat* (*MH* 86). Though never as prominent, suspicion about Thomas's use of sources has never really died down, most recently surfacing again in reviews of his 1998 biography of Solzhenitsyn which argue that the book relies heavily on Michael Scammell's earlier biography (though the debt is acknowledged by Thomas).

Besides his alleged plagiarism, two other aspects of Thomas's fiction have consistently provoked outrage: its approach to sex and its appropriation of some of the most violent episodes in twentieth-century history. Feminists have complained that *The White Hotel* is no more than the author's

3

sadistic fantasy dressed up as an exploration of his heroine's masochistic sexuality. In the most forceful critique, Susanne Kappeler claimed that *The White Hotel* exposed Thomas as 'the snuff artist of the literary establishment'.[6] Other critics have objected to incidental details in his work, like the (admittedly outrageous) disfigured nun masturbating with the remote control over the Zapruder film in his fictional account of the Kennedy assassination, *Flying in to Love* (1992). Similar suspicions have been voiced about Thomas's appropriation of the Holocaust, and in particular the way it is juxtaposed, in novels like *The White Hotel*, *Ararat* and *Pictures at an Exhibition* (1993), with deep eroticism. His depiction of violence, the charge goes, borders on the pornographic: offering lurid and sensational depictions of history to excite his readers and feed his own obsessions rather than seriously address relevant issues of representation.

Thomas has mounted impassioned defences against all of the allegations. But let us put these aside for the moment and consider something significant about the three main areas of objection to Thomas's work – plagiarism, misogyny, and exploitation of the Holocaust. It is striking how all the charges sooner or later come back to the persona of the author himself. The concern with the representation of women in his work has become, over the years, increasingly difficult to separate from a prurient interest in his character and behaviour. This was taken to its most extreme level in 1993 when Thomas was the victim of a pointless journalistic 'honeytrap', when a writer working for the *Modern Review* went to his home disguised as a creative-writing student, then published a damning article on her return.[7] His use of Holocaust material has been seen as a calculated way of securing financial gain or as pandering to his own sado-masochistic fantasies. In the minor media storm which followed the publication of *Pictures at an Exhibition*, a sequel of sorts to *The White Hotel*, the novel was described as 'a cold and calculated piece of writing . . . designed to make its author a great deal of money'.[8]

In one sense, this focus on the author rather than the work is not surprising, for books dealing so prominently with two of the most emotive areas in our culture, sexuality and the Holocaust, frequently spark off debates about the author's motivations.[9] And it has to be said that as much as scandal seems to stick to Thomas, he flirts with it too. He once claimed that when asked by his American publishers how he wanted to mark the launch of the paperback version of *The White Hotel* he asked for 'a cabaret-style dancer bursting out of a cake' (LC 13) – a gesture hardly likely to have eased the controversy brewing over the content of the novel. His memoir *Memories and Hallucinations* (1988) is so honest about his sexual escapades that it borders at times on exhibitionism, and directly fed into the *Guardian*'s caricature of him as a 'Devilish Misogynist' (a play on his trademark initials) in its ironic thumbnail sketch series *Passnotes* in 1993. What is notable, though, is that underlying all of the accusations and interest in his personality is an implicit desire to characterize Thomas in a particular way: as a literary *impostor*.

This is most clear in the case of plagiarism. Thomas was alarmed by the readiness of some contributors to the *TLS* debate to depart from the issues in question and simply 'unleash aggression' towards him.[10] The same impulse seems to have fired the ludicrous and unsubstantiated Grigson and Walker charges. But none of the accusations have ever led to any apologies or retractions. *The White Hotel* acknowledges its debt to Kuznetsov not only on its copyright page, but also in the text.[11] This means that whatever offence Thomas had committed could not really – legally, that is – be plagiarism. The doubts about his translations were equally curious, for as Thomas pointed out, the claim to originality surely rests with the poets being translated; the sense and the language of the poems are theirs rather than their translators's.[12] In fact, Thomas has always scrupulously acknowledged the sources from which he has been accused of borrowing unfairly – this refusal to 'hide' perhaps ironically provoking some of the charges.[13] In reality, in the plagiarism debates Thomas was being accused of something worse than plagiarism: failing in his duty as a novelist to be original and imaginative and, in the words of one accuser, 'sidestepping the labour of the translator'.[14] The accusations, in other words, were primarily motivated – whether or not intentionally – by the desire to expose Thomas as masquerading as someone he is not: just as he had capitalized on emotive cultural issues like the Holocaust to elevate his own status as an author, so he had stolen from others to compensate for his inadequacies as novelist and translator.

The irony here is that the idea of masquerade is actually the perfect metaphor to explain the effects of Thomas's fiction – though it has nothing to do with covering up his literary shortcomings. D. M. Thomas *is* an impostor, but only in the sense that all authors are impostors. What was really at stake in the plagiarism controversies, as Linda Hutcheon recognizes in her article 'Literary Borrowing . . . and Stealing', were two very different conceptions of authorship.[15] Thomas was being judged against the Romantic ideal of the author as a unique individual capable of original imagination and expression, an ideal which is intimately bound up with the capitalist emphasis on ownership and copyright emerging at the same time as Romanticism (around the turn of the nineteenth century). Over the last three decades or so, however, this Romantic conception of authorship, though it is still pervasive in our culture, has been powerfully challenged by literary theory. The conflation of the terms 'ownership' and 'originality' occasioned by the acceleration of capitalism means that the label 'author', as Molly Nesbit has said, had nothing to do with 'supreme distinction, nor did it designate a particular profession, like poet. It was only meant to distinguish a particular kind of labour from another, the cultural from the industrial'.[16] Thus 'plagiarism' (as a number of contributors to the *TLS* symposium during *The White Hotel* controversy pointed out) is a legal category rather than a literary one – a fact which explains why debates about literary plagiarism tend to focus only on the duplication of the actual words of a particular text, not its style nor ideas, and why very few cases of plagiarism ever reach the courts.

The link between authorship and originality has been questioned in other ways too. Theory has taught us that literary composition, rather than being a matter of individual genius (though genius plays a part), is really a complex process of selecting from the network of previously available conventions and discourses (Roland Barthes), or re-interpreting or 'misreading' influential works already in existence (Harold Bloom).[17] Literature in this recent conception can be summed up by the term 'intertextuality', which refers both to a general condition where all texts refer to other texts rather than external reality, and to the practice of citing and echoing the work of specific precursors. Intertextuality (appropriately enough in Thomas's case) is a kind of *translation* whereby the meanings of the original text are carried into the new one, and added to and altered in return. It is according to this idea of authorship that we must understand D. M. Thomas's work.

His fiction repeatedly flaunts the truth about the significance of intertextuality in authorship, simultaneously reminding us that he is responsible for what follows and that others are too. This is most obviously accomplished by the Author's Note which begins each of his novels, crediting important influences and intertexts within. But more challenging still to conventional (Romantic) notions of authorship is a particular kind of intertextuality which features in his work: Thomas's fiction continually duplicates key intertexts, mimicking and altering them. The centrepiece of *The White Hotel* is not Kuznetsov's text but a faultless imitation of a Freudian case study, into the texture of which Thomas weaves lines taken verbatim from Freud's letters, essays and case studies in a much more cunning way than he builds *Babi Yar* into his own story.[18]

This piece of mimicry was followed by an imitation of Pushkin in *Ararat*, a bawdy amendment to Haggard's *King Solomon's Mines* in *Swallow* (1984), versions of Freud again in *Memories and Hallucinations* (1988) and *Lying Together* (1990), which also contained an impersonation of the nineteenth-century psychiatrist Richard von Krafft-Ebing and, most recently, in *Charlotte* (2000), an alternative version of *Jane Eyre*. This practice of mimicking the voices of other authors is the single most striking feature of Thomas's fiction. He has the ability of the forger to copy someone else's style and voice exactly. Unlike the forger, however, Thomas does not attempt to pass the finished product off as his own, but uses it to create something new.

A more appropriate metaphor is *improvisation*, one which is at the heart of his five-volume sequence *Russian Nights*. *Russian Nights* features numerous acts of literary improvisation by its characters (and of course Thomas himself). Its key intertext is Pushkin's unfinished fragment *Egyptian Nights* (1835), which is included in *Ararat*, the first volume of the quintet. The hero of Pushkin's text, Charsky, is amazed at the abilities of a mysterious Italian *improvisatore* to take 'another man's thoughts' and instantly make them his own, 'as if [he] had conceived them, nursed them and developed them over a long period' (*A* 60). Thomas's work is a reminder that all creation is really this kind of improvisation. Every writer is caught, like the *improvisatore* in *Egyptian Nights*, between 'his own inspiration and a strange external will' (*A* 60), between his individuality and the discursive network which shapes it. Thomas duly goes on to complete *Egyptian Nights* in *Ararat* – capturing Pushkin's voice as surely as he captures Freud's in *The White Hotel* – implying that literary creation depends upon a similar telepathic relationship between writers, one transmitting to the other what he had in mind.

The hint of the supernatural in this idea is quite appropriate. For while Thomas's view of artistic creation is quite foreign to the Romantic notion of authorship in so far as it challenges the idea of the transcendent originary genius, it also subscribes to a traditional ideology of the author which is preserved in Romanticism, where the author, or bard, is suddenly inspired to create art by a strange force apparently originating outside him. Thomas is firmly romantic in this sense, believing that 'A writer doesn't choose his subject matter, he submits to it' (AE 4). This is borne out by the many examples he gives in *Memories and Hallucinations* of the strange coincidences and superstitions which, he feels, have clustered around his work. Dreams, memories, poems he has written and books he has read, all come to impose themselves mysteriously on his creative mind, shaping the work he produces. While writing *The White Hotel*, he says, 'I kept discovering new things about Lisa Erdman. Much that was in her letters to Freud took me by surprise' (*MH* 47).

Literature, in other words, in both its production and reception, is presented as something essentially *uncanny*. Freud's notion of the 'uncanny' explains the phenomenon when something familiar takes on a disturbingly unfamiliar aspect by manifesting itself in an unexpected context. His famous essay on the uncanny is representative of the 'other side' of psychoanalysis, less concerned with pretensions to scientific validity than with pondering the links between the supernatural or mythic areas of human experience. This is the Freud which Thomas responds to – and whom he portrays in *The White Hotel* and *Eating Pavlova* (1994) – and the uncanny is the area of his theory best able to describe the complex effects of Thomas's writing.[19]

The 'doubling' effect created by his imitations of Freud or Charlotte Brontë or Pushkin or Dina Pronicheva is typical of the repetitive mechanism of the uncanny, whereby what seemed to be comfortably settled and determinate (such as Freud's theories, or *Jane Eyre*'s status as an authorized classic) is revealed to be uncertain, open to disturbing reversals or questioning. What is reassuringly familiar about the status and voice of a great author or text becomes infected by an unfamiliar and disturbing element once Thomas has finished 'tampering' with them (to use the term of one unimpressed reviewer of *Charlotte*).[20] In *The Anxiety of Influence* Harold Bloom speaks of the uncanny effect which can occur when a successor poet grapples with the work of a predecessor: the previous work is revised in such a powerful way that it seems as if the later poet, more cunningly even than Borges's Pierre Menard who rewrites Cervantes, has written the work of the earlier. One perceptive reviewer of *The White Hotel* displayed more wisdom than most of the contributions to the plagiarism debate by suggesting that the novel's stormy reception had little to do with the question of sources or even fictionalizing a sensitive historical event. Rather, 'the uneasiness provoked by *The White Hotel* seemed to testify more to a general discomfort with [Thomas's] protean powers of projection and assimilation – his witchery'.[21] Thomas's ability to impersonate other writers is a form of literary 'ventriloquism', a way of throwing his own authorial voice to make it appear as though it is coming from someone else. The traditional suspicion of ventriloquism, reflected in its historical association with witchcraft or possession, can be explained, according to Steven Connor, by the fact that the dissociated voice raises a number of disturbing questions about identity, self-presence, and authority.[22] This is the effect of Thomas's ventriloquism.

This uncanny aspect of Thomas's work is symptomatic of the shift in intellectual and aesthetic sensibility often identified as the move from the 'modern' to the 'postmodern'. One of the major characteristics of postmodernism is its challenge to the conventional understanding of representation as a fairly stable operation dependent on a hierarchy between original and copy. Thomas's 'witchery' highlights the fundamental paradox the French philosopher Jean Baudrillard sees in representation: to imitate something is to copy it, but in such a way that the copy becomes simultaneously real and fake, a reproduction that also takes its place in the world as an entity of equal status to the original. *The White Hotel* is a powerful example of this phenomenon. It is founded on the interplay of two key simulacra: the pastiche of the Freudian case study and the adaptation of the eye-witness account in *Babi Yar*. Both are such accurate copies that the referent seems to disappear: it is possible to learn about, or 'experience' Freud and the Holocaust from these accounts, as if they were deliberate forays into historiography. The effect, Jeffrey Berman says, half admiringly, half uncomfortably, is 'that Thomas' fictional character has influenced the history of psychoanalysis'.[23] Something similar occurs in *Eating Pavlova*, an even more extensive impersonation of Freud. The novel poses as Freud's private diary and contains numerous revelations about the gaps in Freud's biography, such as the nature of his relationships with his wife and sister-in-law. These are blended so intricately with the known facts that after reading the novel, thinking about Freud becomes unavoidably influenced by Thomas's portrayal of him, and details from biography and fiction are easy to confuse.

Thomas's ability to *be* Freud or Pushkin, to play the literary impostor, reminds us of the fragility of the concepts of 'originality' and 'authorship' – and, most of all, of the 'real' itself. The uncanny emerges on occasions when previously stable boundaries are crossed: familiar becomes unfamiliar, something within the self affects the world outside the self, or seems to, the real world appears to take on the characteristics of fiction. The effect of Thomas's work is uncanny in the way it continually addresses, and more powerfully *stages*, the blurring of boundaries, restlessly probing the division between apparently distinctive entities – the notions of voice, authorship, text, genre – as well as interrogating the limits of other fundamentals like the self, memory, life, death and history. To read D. M. Thomas is to be made aware of the web of intertextuality that is literary history: no literary work stands on its own, but is effectively a collaboration between past and present voices. It thus echoes the insights of critical theorists like Bakhtin, Barthes and Kristeva, who have portrayed literature as a *polyphonic* form of discourse, that is, made up of a number of different voices which interact with, contradict and clash with each other. And what leads on from this is that the human subject is constituted just as surely by different voices: those of other people outside the self, and from that 'other' inside us called the unconscious.

This, then, suggests what is really troubling about Thomas's work, and also accounts for his importance in contemporary literature. Studying his fiction and the response to it provides an insight into some of the dominant concerns of both theorists and practitioners of the English novel in the late twentieth century. It is not surprising that the defence against fiction like his which troublingly asserts the fact that authorship is always a matter of masquerade and collaboration should be to substitute the focus on the work for an image of its author as a consistent embodied subject, in which the identity of the writer coincides with that of the man. This is the aim of the plagiarism accusations – to attempt to limit the ventriloquial aspect of Thomas's fiction: whenever he throws his voice and speaks from another position, the attempt is made to return it to its original location, Thomas himself. Ironically, this is an example of a critical approach normally adopted in relation to the work of certain women writers. We could say of the media response to Thomas's work what is typically said about female desire in culture, that the glare of the disturbing elements of his work is reflected back on the author himself, thus containing its subversive potential.

Labelling Thomas a plagiarist, in other words, is a strategy of limitation. We might even describe the accusation that Thomas is a literary pornographer in similar terms. In an influential essay, Susan Sontag has shown how categorizing a work that deals with 'extreme' situations as 'pornography' (or as 'fantasy' or 'science fiction', other derogatory labels) works as a safeguard against its troubling capacity to exceed prescriptive 'realist' standards of fiction. But the obsessive quality of the 'pornographic imagination' in its properly artistic form (as opposed to other, less complex, kinds) contains 'something that touches upon the reader's whole experience of his humanity – and his limits as a personality and as a body'. By doing so it confirms that 'sexuality remains one of the demonic forces in human consciousness – pushing us at intervals close to taboo and dangerous desires, which range from the impulse to commit sudden arbitrary violence upon another person to the voluptuous yearning for the extinction of one's consciousness, for death itself'.[24]

Thomas is certainly a writer who deals in extremes, and has himself acknowledged that his persistent interest in sex and death 'gives my novels an obsessional feel disturbing to many' (AE 4). While it is undoubtedly the case that his portrayal of women is at times problematic (though I think this applies more to the insipid sex scenes in *Russian Nights* or the second half of *Charlotte* than the characterization of Lisa in *The White Hotel* – not because they are offensive so much as because they are stereotypical) what makes the depiction of the extremes of sexuality disturbing to many readers is the way it is juxtaposed – quite legitimately, it seems to me – with equally extreme scenes of death. Sontag's argument suggests that, like the implicit accusation that he is an impostor, there is something accurate in the otherwise oversimplified charge that aspects of Thomas's work are pornographic. Thomas thus both fits and exceeds the labels used to stabilize his identity, just as – so I aim to demonstrate in this book – his extreme fiction gains its power from its continued probing of fundamental boundaries in both art and life.

2

Voices: *Dreaming in Bronze, Birthstone, The Flute-Player*

It is common for writers to speak of 'finding their voice' as their writing develops. It means discovering what is original about their writing, what marks it out from others. But there is something strange, almost uncanny, about the idea too – as if finding what is most true to the self depends upon going beyond it. In his curious, formally inventive autobiography, *Memories and Hallucinations*, Thomas describes coming across his first published work, his only short story, 'The Opportunist', which appeared in 1958 in the Oxford University magazine *Isis*, under the name Donald Thomas. What surprises and moves him most is 'to recognize – despite the Lawrentian echoes – my voice. That didn't happen with most of the execrable early poems I found in the other magazines that tumbled out of the old suitcase. But the prose style – that was me, essentially no different from the man I am now' (*MH* 175). This is a curious observation from someone who has earlier in the same book confessed to not having 'a prose style that is my own' (*MH* 47) and who constantly looks to the styles of other writers to bring a sense of formal restraint to the process of composition. Yet the contradiction reflects the 'doubleness' of Thomas's voice in his fiction. Thomas's voice is 'his' in that it expresses the same obsessions and compulsions which run through all his work. At the same time it demonstrates – in a way that affirms Bakhtin's 'dialogical principle' – that each single voice is actually composed of other voices which act upon it and respond to it.

Donald Michael Thomas was born in 1935 and brought up in Redruth, 'the sadly haunting, wrecked tin-mining area of

13

West Cornwall, its symbol the square ugly granite harmony-filled Wesleyan chapel'.[1] Thomas's father Harold was a tin-miner like his ancestors, and Thomas grew up 'overwhelmingly within the atmosphere of the paternal family', surrounded by aunts and uncles, often living all together in 'the tribal house' (*MH* 148). Thomas's account of his home life in *Memories and Hallucinations* gives an impression of nourishing serenity and calmness, a sheltered world which kept him from visiting a pub until he was 24, even though he had served in the Army by that time.[2] But Thomas also saw himself as an 'outsider within', partly because he was the only young person in the family (he was born when his parents were in their 30s, had a much older sister, and was surrounded by older relatives), partly because of what he regards as his peculiar predisposition towards complexity instead of the simple virtues his family life was founded upon. These are standard artist credentials of course, and Thomas recognizes that his 'detachment' from his family partly shaped his vocation.[3] He started out as a poet, publishing his first collection, *Personal and Possessive*, in 1964.

In his preface to his first volume of *Selected Poems*, issued in 1983 to capitalize on his fame after *The White Hotel*, Thomas identifies the 'primary emotional landscape' of his poetry as Cornwall.[4] The phrase 'emotional landscape' suggests a link between psychic and geographical space which is central to his work. It is visible in the places which give their names to his novels, like the strange resort in *The White Hotel*, Mount Ararat, and Love Field airport where the Kennedys landed before the assassination (*Flying in to Love*), as well as in the many journeys, usually by train or boat, which recur throughout his fiction and poetry, and which combine a literal journey with a metaphorical one, into the depths of the unconscious, personal and collective.

In his poems, though, there is something we do not find in his novels: a specific sense of *embodiment* in Cornwall, as if the location and the people who inhabit it are made of the same material. His poetry often deals with the Cornish past, in both its ancient Celtic form, represented by the monuments or places which give many of the poems titles ('Logan Stone', 'Botallack' or 'Penwith'), and in a concern with its more recent tin-mining history ('A Cornish Graveyard in Keenaw', 'The Shaft'). To use the imagery of 'The Shaft', a meditation on the Cornish miners who periodically travelled around the world to find work (usually to America, like his own parents), it is as if Thomas is burrowing into the very landscape to get in touch with his origins. Most often the poems achieve this by focusing on members of his immediate family, especially his parents. In 'The Journey',[5] for example, a silent car trip leaves Thomas meditating on how closely bound up his life is with his mother's and with the Cornish landscape: 'For we are water and moor,/ And far journeyers together' (lines 38–9).

One of the many outstanding poems in Thomas's 1981 collection, *Dreaming in Bronze*, is 'The Handkerchief or Ghost Tree', a moving account of a visit taken by the adult Thomas with his family to the garden of Glendurgan in Cornwall. The trip reminds him of Durgan beach, where he himself had been taken as a boy: he is carrying a child in his arms, just as he himself had been carried in his father's. After identifying the Handkerchief or Ghost tree, there in the garden amidst many other kinds of tree, he is moved to consider the 'ghosts' of his parents: his mother, who once saw a ghost warning her of the death of Thomas's father, and his father himself, whose knotted handkerchief, 'still wringing with the sweat/ I had watched pour out of him' (lines 24–5), Thomas found when collecting his father's clothes from hospital after his death. Perhaps there is even the ghost of himself as a child. We suddenly switch to an image of a small boy running into the garden and vanishing, who is at once Thomas's young son Ross running on into the maze and the earlier incarnation of himself conjured up by his moment of reflection. He can hear this ghost-child's voice and glimpse his face through the leaves. The poem ends with a moving image of the trees in the garden, which come to represent the ghosts of people all knitted together in a huddle stretching through history, linking generations, time, and nationalities:

> These lives . . . these lives that come
> and go mysteriously, as the laurel leaves
> shine and gloom in the cloudy
> sunlight through the tall trees,

this convocation of
the world's trees, massing now
into one, without losing their distinct
character, in the walk down to Durgan.

(lines 38–45)

This idea of a ghostly calling together is a particularly appropriate one for Thomas. 'The Handkerchief or Ghost Tree' meditates on the importance of family lines and on the merging of different voices – two of the principle themes of his poetry.

Until *Dreaming in Bronze*, Thomas himself is curiously absent from his poetry. Personal significance is strongly implied, of course, by the continued concern with his ancestral past, but a direct reflection of his own experience is usually missing. Where Thomas reproduces the voices of dead relatives in poems like 'Under Carn Brea' and the beautiful 'The Honeymoon Voyage', his 'own' voice, speaking directly about himself, is more elusive. This absence can perhaps be explained by the fact that, as he himself felt, much of his earlier work had tended to be 'over-elaborate, too intellectual, too cerebral' (DW 37). *Dreaming in Bronze*, by contrast, figures as a sustained poetic inquiry into himself. One of the most important poems in the collection is 'Big Deaths, Little Deaths', an autobiography in key episodes, all of which (as the title suggests) are underscored by death or sex: his sexual awakening, his adolescence in Australia, the death of his father. In his preface to *Selected Poems* Thomas claims that 'all my poems take issue with love and death',[6] and this is something he has reiterated many times over the years, in relation to his novels as well. There is no doubt in his mind, either, about the formative period of his life. The brief time he spent in Australia is returned to again and again in interviews, his memoir, and in the novel *Swallow*, like a Freudian 'primal scene'. This period marked the major 'firsts' in his life: first time away from Cornwall, first wet dream, first love, first music, first poetry.[7]

It is the setting for another major poem in *Dreaming in Bronze*, 'The Puberty Tree', where Thomas remembers nights lying in his bed during the intense summer heat of Melbourne, yet frozen in terror at the sight of the huge shadowy tree outside his window. All the emerging desires and anxieties of

16

adolescence are projected onto the tree, as he imagines the swaying branches casting a great spider (Thomas is an arachnaphobe) into the room. The encounter with the spider crystallizes the fears and desires which will shape the course of his life – and work – to come, planting them firmly inside him and making the tree, in turn, an outward reflection of his own personality:

> Night by night the tree went on spinning black
> and white substances into me;
> now it is wholly inside me: my groin the root,
> the slender bough my spine, the saw-edged leaves
> my imagination; and the tree sways between
> the dark, the light.
>
> (lines 23–8)

For Thomas, it seems, the adult is formed in puberty rather than early childhood. The significance of the poem is emphasized by the fact that Thomas used it as the title of his second volume of collected poems, published in 1992.

Dreaming in Bronze, then, is the collection where Thomas really 'finds his voice' in his poetry. It also sees an increase in another kind of poem he has always specialized in: the dramatic monologue which reanimates a historical figure. Dramatic monologues feature heavily in his first full collection, called, appropriately enough, *Two Voices* (1968), where they display an impressive ability to reproduce the speech of a certain recognizable *kind* of person and the worldview attached to it. Yet the early dramatic monologues remain strangely 'cold' poems, somewhat obscure and private. *Dreaming in Bronze*, however, demonstrates a mature mastery of the form, presenting a series of poems lined up together like animated statues. Thomas reproduces the voices of Pushkin ('Farewell, My Life; I Love You'), Pushkin's version of Don Juan ('The Stone Guest'), Freud and his disciples in 'Fathers, Sons and Lovers', Freud's famous patient 'The Wolf Man', and the notorious 1920s German serial killer Peter Kürten.

In one sense these poems can be seen as rehearsals for *The White Hotel*, in that the lengthy impersonation of Freud which forms the centrepiece of that novel emerged from the same creative spring. More generally, though, the practice of revitalizing 'dead' voices in Thomas's last few collections of poetry seems to have enabled him to develop his ability to impersonate others.

This is something he was already aware of as a result of his experiences as a translator. *Dreaming in Bronze* is clearly, on one level, Thomas's response to translating Pushkin, which he was doing while writing his own poems. Thomas describes translation as a mysterious process, almost mystical rather than technical. 'Poem in a Strange Language' (1975), for example, contains the lines

> I enter your poem, Mandelstam, yours, Anna
> Akhmatova, as I enter my love –
> Without understanding anything
> Except its beauty and law.
>
> (lines 13–16)

'Portraits' imagines a dialogue with Akhmatova, while 'Poem of the Midway' envisages a meeting with Marina Tsvetaeva ('Anywhere in Europe/ and our century will be dark/ enough for our assignation', lines 43–5). This is Thomas's experience of literary history, where the voices of the living speak with and reanimate those of the dead. As a metaphor for Thomas's writing, in fact, translation rivals impersonation or improvisation. He is a translator in what we might regard as the full sense of the term, someone who becomes possessed by the words or ideas or drama of someone else, and translates them into other contexts and other 'languages'.

Dreaming in Bronze can be read as a work about the existential implications of simultaneously finding one's own voice and finding the voices of others. This perhaps explains why it is not only Thomas's best collection of poetry but also his last to date. Shortly after it (and *The White Hotel*) had appeared he entered into a period of being blocked, realizing that he 'couldn't write a straight novel; but [. . .] couldn't write a straight poem any more either' (*MH* 56). This undoubtedly had much to do with the peculiar pressures which came from the 'triple division' within his writing – that is, being a poet, novelist and translator concurrently (DW 37). To resolve the problem, Thomas decided after *Dreaming in Bronze* to concentrate almost exclusively on the novel.

This points to an obvious temptation for anyone writing on his work, as it seems Thomas's career can be divided neatly into two phases, poetry then fiction, like a Thomas Hardy in reverse. Yet this is misleading. His fiction continually destabilizes the notion of genre, and much of *Russian Nights*, the quintet of novels which followed *Dreaming in Bronze*, is made up of lengthy sections of narrative poetry. Thomas has long protested his discomfort with 'rigid classification': 'I would like to turn back to the ancient simplicity in which any maker with words was a poet'.[8] Nevertheless Thomas was reluctant to write novels for many years, claiming to have no special feeling for the form. Paradoxically, he is a novelist whose very reluctance to be one leads him to conceive of the fictional innovations which make him a writer of note. But his initial indifference towards the novel, as he realized himself, was really a distaste for 'the typical *English* novel, in which a few characters have love affairs, one or two get married or die – and you think, at the end of it, "So what?" ' (my italics).[9] It was only when he discovered, rather belatedly, through writers like Turgenev, Pasternak, Joyce, and especially Mikhail Bulgakov in *The Master and Margarita* (1966–7), that a different, poetic kind of novel was possible, one 'in which you get a mixture of lyricism and swift narrative' (*MH* 18), that Thomas took the idea of writing a novel seriously. He conceived of writing fiction which would 'follow the creative laws of poetry, based very largely on symbol and image'.[10] Thomas has described the process of writing a novel in distinctly poetic terms:

> I can only get to grips with a novel when there is some kind of *symbol* at work, and therefore when it suddenly takes on a multiplicity of meanings – whether it's the birthstone, or a bare room with a woman in it, or a railway carriage and a white hotel. [. . .] I imagine most novelists feel they've got a novel when they've got a couple of convincing characters and a plot. But I can't write like that. I'm not really interested in exploring motivation. I need an image that is capable of expanding, and then individual words, enriched by association with that central image. (DW 34)

He alludes to his first three novels here, but his comments apply to almost all of the novels which follow, which are often named after the central image which feeds them: *Ararat, Swallow, Sphinx, Flying in to Love*.

Thomas's first novel was *Birthstone*, published in 1980. It began with the 'central image' of an ancient Cornish monument, the Men-an-tol, a stone ring which people used to pass through to cure illnesses. The novel is about 'a trinity of odd characters, sick in different ways' (*MH* 19) who follow this custom and find the experience affects them radically. Hector Bolitho, an astronomer, has brought his mother Lola to Cornwall to visit the home she has never seen before she dies. On the bus they meet Jo, a neurotic Irishwoman, who is on holiday to recuperate. After crawling through the birthstone they decide to live together for a while in a cottage nearby. This place turns into the kind of 'resort' Thomas depicts in *The White Hotel*: an atmosphere of 'holiday' reigns (the novel could be analysed in terms of Bakhtin's idea of 'carnival'), everyday social and sexual laws appear to be suspended, inhibitions are removed, desires are freely expressed and fulfilled. Hector begins to age drastically, while Lola does just the opposite, becoming younger and rediscovering her zest for life, ending the novel as an adolescent. Increasingly Jo is 'taken over' by the different personalities who dwell in her troubled psyche. The characters flirt and have sex with each other more and more indiscriminately. This is the first treatment of a theme we often find in Thomas, which explores the powerful transformative potential of an unchecked flow of libidinal energy. As the imagery makes abundantly clear (as does the poem most obviously related to the novel, 'Penwith' from the 1971 collection *Logan Stone*), the ring-like birthstone figures as a vagina, representing what Thomas sees as the 'feminine' principles of restorative creativity and myth, which challenge the ordered social world (*MH* 19).

In an obvious sense, the novel is the most autobiographical of Thomas's fictions, more so even than *Lying Together* a novel in which he himself actually appears. In that novel, there is little of Thomas's past. *Birthstone*, by contrast, is set in a Cornish landscape which evokes some of the mythic past explored in Thomas's poetry, thus legitimating the fantasy space opened up by the characters' passage through the stone. Thomas has explicitly linked his interest in fantasy and dreams to his Celtic background: 'Celts are very superstitious, possessing a great sense of another world haunting our own. I guess I share in that'.[11] His work is Celtic, he thinks, in so far as it is concerned with 'eroticism and the feminine' and the confusion of 'the borders between fantasy and reality, life and death' (*MH* 126).[12] Certainly, the sensibility of *Birthstone* is reminiscent of the typical Celtic blend of exuberant energy and more down-to-earth realism.

A more specific pointer to Thomas's own history is the fact that Hector and Lola are based in part on his parents. Both are Cornish exiles living in California, just as Thomas's parents had spent some time in Los Angeles in their early married life. This comparison extends onto a psychological level, as the couple are also representative of Thomas's own formative Oedipal triangle. As he has described them himself, Hector and Lola's roles alternate between mother and son, husband and wife, father and daughter (*MH* 20), thus amounting to a – no doubt partly ironic – playing out of his own Oedipal fantasies. Because Hector gets older as Lola gets younger, the author can participate in the aspects of his parents's relationship to which he was not privy (*MH* 9), and indulge in some wish-fulfilment around the fantasy figure of his mother. *Memories and Hallucinations* and many of Thomas's poems testify to the intensity of his love for his mother, and also to the real reversal of roles which occurred late in her life when Thomas had to care for her, like father to child.

Psychopathology is as central to this text as it will be in later novels. Jo suffers from Multiple Personality Disorder, a condition which develops out of the need to protect oneself from early trauma by filing the traumatic memory away in the fantasmatic consciousnesses of a range of fictitious personae. Like the most famous case, that of 'Sybil', analysed by Flora Rheta Schreiber[13] (mentioned in *Birthstone*), Jo is menaced by a number of alter egos, the uninhibited Joanne, the censorious bully Joe, the nostalgic mature Joan, etc., who 'take over' her personality without warning, seducing or attacking other chararacters and then leaving Jo to explain 'their' actions, and writing to her continually in letters, postcards, and poems. MPD bears clear links with the ideas of 'split personality' and possession common in folklore, mythology and literature. Its

21

treatment in *Birthstone* clearly relates to one of Thomas's keenest interests. Making Joanne a split personality, Thomas has said, 'did seem to reflect what the artist is doing all the time: what the novelist is doing particularly. The novelist is very much a split personality; otherwise he couldn't work' (DW 28).

Indeed, the idea of the split personality is seldom far from the surface whenever Thomas has discussed the experience of being an author. Ever since being pitched into celebrity by *The White Hotel*, he has been painfully aware of the division between the person he feels he really is and the man his readers expect him to be, whether that is the cultured figure of the 'serious' author (LC), or the lecherous and 'sordidly commercial' 'Devilish Misogynist' (AE 4). He has described the very process of writing in similar terms: becoming conscious of an authorial double, 'a brooding, obsessional figure, bearing my name, who paces rooms and eventually darts towards the word processor' once inspired (AE 4). Writerly doubles are a recurring concern in Thomas's work and life. *Russian Nights* is full of them, and even the initialled name which appears on the covers of his books is explained by the fact that a contemporary at Oxford in the late 1950s was also called Donald Thomas and he happened to publish a volume of poems first: 'I have been haunted by him ever since: often I am complimented for a poem I didn't write, or my scholarly book on censorship' (*MH* 32).

While *Birthstone* is not overtly about writing, as many of Thomas's novels are, the related concern with the interpenetration of voices and consciousnesses is central. Though Jo is the only character to have a name for her condition, she is not the only one whose identity is fractured. Lola undergoes a more subtle transmutation into another person, taking on the character of the notorious nineteenth-century dancer Lola Montez, similarly offending morality and shocking people wherever she goes with her exhibitionist exploits. An experience of commingling voices governed the composition of the novel, which was originally planned as the product of two writers, Thomas and the poet Elizabeth Ashworth. When Ashworth had to withdraw at an early stage due to pressure of work, Thomas was not too disappointed, for he had already 'developed a maternal love for it, and wanted it in my womb' (*MH* 19). But it meant that Thomas had to assimiliate Ashworth's voice into his own (or vice versa) because 'We had chosen a setting familiar to me, west Cornwall, and a "voice" familiar to her – a female narrator' (*MH* 19).

What makes the treatment of polyphony most powerful is the way Thomas uses the form of the novel to accentuate it. Unlike the impersonations in his dramatic monologues, the various fractured voices are knitted together seamlessly, but in a way which ultimately reinforces rather than dilutes the idea of fragmentation. We can see this in a typical instance where Jo switches between personalities without warning:

> One moment I was crying about the news from Aberfan, strapped up as usual without being consciously so, and the next I was at a party jiving to 'Sergeant Pepper', with a panicky feeling that my suspender belt had broken. I looked down and saw I was in this indecently short skirt, and some kind of Shakespearean tights. Then a second panic: I'd forgotten my bra. My surprise at this liberation was quickly overtaken by the knowledge, picked up from Joanne's friends, that my father had died during the intervening months. I felt, in every way, unsupported. (*B* 67)

The effect is disorienting for the reader, who cannot easily attribute the different perspectives to particular consciousnesses. Thomas's narration of events in the novel suggests how the real world appears when drunk, dreaming, or drugged: it is recognizably the everyday world, but specific elements can be grotesquely overemphasized or foregrounded at any moment. All of the action of *Birthstone* takes place in a world which is analogous to the real world but frequently departs from its laws of social restraint. It becomes increasingly difficult to keep track of what is 'really' happening in the main story. The form of the novel, in this sense, mirrors what we might see as the 'phenomenology' of psychopathology – the way the world really presents itself to the mind during neurotic or psychotic hallucination. The most powerful element of *Birthstone*, in other words, is the way it breaks down the boundaries between self and world, making it unclear which events are occurring outside the mind. It thus presents the self as a fragmentary, fractured organism, multiple rather than unitary, in process rather than fixed – as incoherent as the real world in which it is placed.

Thomas intended *Birthstone* to be his only excursion into the novel, a temporary escape from poetry (*MH* 18). Yet once it was finished, 'maddeningly, an idea for another novel took hold of me and wouldn't let me go' (*MH* 20). *The Flute-Player* was written in a flurry of activity, the finished result more or less its first draft (DW 29). Along with *Birthstone*, it was entered for the 1979 Gollancz/Picador/Guardian Fantasy Competition. It won, and was published in 1979 before *Birthstone*, which eventually appeared the next year. Both novels can be related to the fantastic in the sense which Tzvetan Todorov has defined the term, dividing it into two key modes: the *marvellous*, where unreal events happen but are accepted as entirely normal within the world of the fiction, and the *uncanny*, where unreal events are the product of processes like dreams, hallucinations, or delusions at work in the psyche of the narrator or characters from whose viewpoint the story is being told.[14] Where *Birthstone* conforms to this latter category (resembling in particular the tradition of Menippean satire, a form favoured by Russian authors like Dostoevsky and Gogol), *The Flute-Player* resembles the former. In particular it corresponds to the distinctive subdivision of the marvellous known as 'magic realism', in which fantastic events are combined with real events narrated in the objective, rationalistic tone of the conventional realist narrator, often to service a strongly political motivation.

The Flute-Player tells the story of Elena, who lives in a single room of a decaying apartment building. She is the flute-player of the title, 'the Muse, all the more powerful for not knowing it' (*MH* 21). Despite facing some terrible hardship and brutality at the hands of the repressive authorities or violent men, she nourishes a variety of artists (male and female) either by being the inspiration for their work or by having sex with them. All this takes place against a background of everyday life in a totalitarian state, a world of parcel bombs, threatening state decrees, unexplained arrests, mysterious murders, ghettos, which occasionally strikes a phantasmagoric note: 'Limbs, long unburied, stuck out of deep snow. Long-dead hands implored mercy. Decapitated heads, stuck on pikes, adorned one of the bridges' (*FP* 29). Elena is put in prison for prostitution and listens to terrified screams, 'unclear whether [they] belonged to other women or herself' (*FP* 50). The story is episodic rather than plotted, concentrating more on depicting the rhythms of totalitarian society, where periods of relatively comfortable normality are punctuated by intermittent renewals of state brutality.

Though the novel is careful never to name the city or the country in which it is set (and wards off attempts to guess, by ensuring that the city at one point has two names, like St Petersburg/Leningrad (*FP* 121) but also a great wall built to divide it, like Berlin (*FP* 143)) it is clear that the book is about Russia. The dedication page salutes the memory of Akhmatova, Osip Mandelstam, Boris Pasternak and Marina Tsvetaeva, the four poets referred to in Akhmatova's delirious poem 'There are Four of Us', all of whom were central to the 'Silver Age' of Russian creativity which flourished against considerable state oppression in the early part of the century. Thomas regards Russia as the 'secondary emotional landscape' of his work, after Cornwall; though he encountered it 'only through its language and literature', it became a second homeland. He conceives of links between the two: their 'atmospheric contrasts',[15] the Granite city of Petersburg and the granite landscape of Cornwall (*MH* 86) and the shared 'emotionalism' of the Celts and the Slavs.[16] Thomas learned Russian while serving in the Army in the early 1950s, where, as he has often pointed out with relish, the future translator of Pushkin was graded by his training officers as 'suitable for low-level interrogation of prisoners'. Though he was never required to interrogate anyone, the experience instilled in Thomas a feeling for Russian culture (*MH* 87). This lay dormant within him until the 1970s, where the importance of Russia first makes itself known in his poetry and his translations of Akhmatova and Pushkin, perhaps its two greatest poets.

Part of the fascination Russia holds for Thomas is its status as supreme representative of the most violent continent and the most violent century in history: 'Russia is a convenience for Western writers', he has said, 'If Dante were alive today he wouldn't have to invent hell' (*MH* 57). A consequence of this is what he perceives as a different approach to literature in Russia than in more politically stable countries. There is the feeling among writers and readers in Russia that literature 'really *does* matter – which I find lacking in a lot of English literature, where it's almost a kind of sport – very nice, but an extra' (DW 36). Thomas regards the line of great Russian writers which began with Pushkin as 'more than writers; they were, since they all lived under authoritarian or tyrannical regimes, "another government" in Solzhenitsyn's phrase: cherished by their fellow Russians because they felt a special responsibility to be truthful'.[17] The torturous experience of being an artist in Russia accounts, too, for the particular appeal of the fantastic to its writers. Todorov suggests that fantasy in literature increases as culture becomes more positivistic and materialist, functioning as a kind of shadow of the rationalism of the dominant political ideology. By inverting the real, Russian fantasy demonstrates that there is something deeply strange and disturbing at the heart of what we are expected to accept as normality. This is the way the fantasy works in *The Flute-Player*, as the novel demonstrates how close the *realities* of totalitarian life come to articulating the fears, impulses toward brutality and sexual desire which dwell in the unconscious. It depicts totalitarianism as Freud saw it, as a phenomenon which enabled individual psychopathic tendencies to be played out on a collective scale. At one point, Elena, who has returned to her periodic occupation as prostitute is troubled to find that 'As if sensing some new and greater disaster round the corner, her customers' taste for sensation and perversity was growing ever more acute' (FP 97).

But Russian literature is also no more than a particularly extreme example of the tension we find in all societies between the strict repressive law and the impulse towards dissension and freedom represented by art. It is worth remembering that Thomas emerged as a novelist at the beginning of the 1980s (like many of the most important British writers of the late twentieth century), the start of one of the most ideologically powerful and suppressive régimes modern Britain has ever seen. While keen to avoid exaggeration, Thomas has pointed out the similarities between the overt harassment of artists in totalitarian régimes and the 'undercurrent of censorship' he has faced in the responses to his work.[18] This explains Thomas's reluctance to claim that *The Flute-Player* is purely about Russia, despite that country's special significance. Rather the novel is essentially 'a micro-history of *all* time ... both a microcosm of the twentieth century, but also in another way of all centuries – writers throughout the centuries, and indeed woman throughout time' (DW 30).

This comment alerts us to the fact that, for all its generality, the novel sees one writer in particular as representing the essence of the poetic spirit which endures in the face of brutal totalitarian philistinism. Once the 'germinal' image of *The Flute-Player* – a 'bleak, naked room with a woman in it' (DW 40) – had come to him, Thomas's mind turned to Anna Akhmatova, who 'spent most of her life cooped up in one room on the Neva embankment; around her swirled the evil tide of history; she was witness to all its crimes' (*MH* 20–21). When many intellectuals and writers fled Russia in the aftermath of the revolution, Akhmatova chose to stay and 'bear witness'. 'Can it be by chance', Thomas has asked, 'that the worst of times found the best of poets to wage the war for eternal truth and human dignity?'[19]

Akhmatova is one of Thomas's key influences. She is the kind of instinctive Romantic poet he most admires, who often became 'possessed' by a poem she was writing.[20] Translating her, Thomas found his own poetic style 'purified by these sorties into the studio of a great artist' (*MH* 89). Her importance to him is such that it surpasses simply her poetic or heroic quality. He has described her as 'a kind of white witch ... pagan and spiritual', the embodiment of Woman, the 'conscience of Russia'.[21] One of his poems, called 'Muse', is about waiting for Akhmatova to come at night, 'flute in hand' and inspire him (*MH* 89). This relates directly to the end of *The Flute-Player*, when the third-person narration gives way to a first-person narrator who intrudes on Elena as she practises her flute by the window. Aware someone has crept in, she turns and looks enigmatically at the author. It also connects to comments Thomas has made about his method of composition. Writing, he maintains, 'is definitely a feminine activity ... There has to be a lot of intuition ... you have to be passive in a way, you have to be receptive, to draw upon your own unconscious and outside influences, just let them swim around and then they kind of settle'.[22] Thomas is evoking here (as he has done on other occasions, e.g. *MH* 19) Jung's notion of the anima, 'a personification of all feminine psychological tendencies in a man's psyche, such as vague feelings and moods, prophetic hunches, receptiveness to the irrational, capacity for personal love, feeling for nature and – last but not least – his relation to the unconscious'.[23] *The Flute-Player* is about Akhmatova, and therefore also about Thomas's own process of composition.

Akhmatova, whom Thomas imagines as his muse, is the most important writer referred to by the novel, but by no means the only one. It begins with a note from the author announcing that 'Quotations ascribed in this novel to two of the fictional characters are from: Akhmadulina, Akhmatova, Baudelaire, Chapman, Dante, Emily Dickinson, Eliot, Frost, Lorca, Mandelstam, Nadezhda Mandelstam, Pasternak, Sylvia Plath, Pushkin, Rilke, Anne Sexton, Shakespeare, Gaspara Stampa, Tsvetaeva, and Yeats. May they forgive the author for these misappropriations and distortions.' This enigmatic announcement serves as a declaration of intent, on two levels. Most obviously, it suggests that Thomas deliberately seeks to place his writing in the context of literature outside Britain (only Shakespeare and Chapman are English, only Eliot, Yeats and Plath associated with British poetry). In fact his work is seldom concerned with class in the way that many of his contemporaries are (even though he followed a familiar pattern for writers of his generation, going to Oxford in 1955 on a scholarship to study English Literature), nor is it afraid of dealing head on with the body and sex (menstruation is part of the symbolic framework of both *Birthstone* and *The Flute-Player*). This comes in contrast to the many English writers who think that sex should be treated 'from a cool, ironic distance, but it should not carry any suggestion of the numinous, as it does in Yeats, Joyce, Dylan Thomas, and earlier Celtic writers and storytellers' (*MH* 131). But besides its implicit concern with the British novel, the announcement at the beginning of *The Flute-Player* figures as Thomas's first explicit indication of the intertextual method so central to his work. It suggests that he has deliberately set out to blend historical reality with fiction without making the divisions clear. It is at once specific and vague, carefully referencing each relevant poet, but not feeling any need to enlighten readers about the extent of his borrowings, where exactly they can be found in his text, and what precisely his 'misappropriation and distortion' has entailed. It is no easy matter determining which of *The Flute-Player*'s characters represent particular poets. The character Michael, for example, writes a poem, like Yeats, about a 'slouching beast' (*FP* 106), but is also a friend of a poet who had jumped to her death like Tsvetaeva (*FP* 40).

The acknowledgement has nothing to do with copyright and everything to do with the true literary – rather than legal – understanding of 'influence'. Writing is subtly envisaged in *The Flute-Player* as the product of a kind of transglobal, transhistorical community of artists, underlining the fact that Thomas's attitude to influence is less a matter of anxiety than open dependence. Yet deliberate vagueness on the part of a writer about the nature or extent of his borrowings is guaranteed to instil anxiety in those keen to keep one author's voice – and identity – separate from another. This would be clear from the response to Thomas's next novel, *The White Hotel*, the extraordinary power of which comes from Thomas even more extensively blending his own voice with others, allowing the voice in his unconscious (the anima or muse), and those of other writers, to speak through him.

3

The Art of Seduction: *The White Hotel*

The White Hotel's capacity to generate critical readings is remarkable by any standards, but especially striking given the comparative neglect of Thomas's other work. Over fifty academic articles and chapters in many languages have been devoted to the novel, while there is next to nothing on anything else he has written.[1] Its potential for interpretation took Thomas by surprise: 'When I had finished my novel, I viewed it rather as if it was a vase that I had made; illogically I expected others to look at the vase and see the same shape. But when it was published, it turned out not to be a well-wrought urn but more like a bolt of energy, which flashed around unpredictably, and appeared in a different form to different people' (LC 8). That readers should be seduced into trying to decode the novel is quite understandable, however, for its rich symbolic form begs interpretation even while its story documents a disturbing failure of interpretation. Some, as I have suggested, have attempted to close down the number of meanings the novel produces by focusing on its author – his attitude to women, violence, psychoanalysis, artistic originality. As a result Thomas has been forced repeatedly into explaining its motivations and techniques – offering what ·amounts to an 'authorized' interpretation (see e.g. the *TLS* debate, SL, LC, *MH*). This is ironic, for the energy of *The White Hotel* derives above all from the way it challenges the idea of authority in reading and writing.

The White Hotel tells the story of Lisa Erdman, a 29-year-old opera singer who goes to Sigmund Freud for analysis in the autumn of 1919 suffering from what appear to be acute hysterical symptoms: severe pains in her left breast and her pelvic region, chronic breathlessness, hallucinations of disaster – a flood, a hotel fire, falling through the air to her death, mourners being buried in a landslide. Following the death of Freud's daughter Sophie, in January 1920, which Lisa has uncannily predicted in a dream (while also foreseeing the later death of his grandson Heinz), Freud suspends her treatment. After taking a break at the resort of Bad Gastein, during which her symptoms seem to be in remission, she gives Freud a long narrative poem written between the staves of the score for Mozart's opera *Don Giovanni*. The poem is an erotic fantasy which begins with an unbridled sexual encounter between Lisa and Freud's son Martin on a train and ends in a hotel in an idyllic mountain landscape against a background of the kind of catastrophic events which feature in her hallucinations. Fascinated, Freud asks her to write down an interpretation of the poem. Instead she brings him a more elaborate prose version of the same story. Freud describes her writings as 'an extreme of libidinous phantasy combined with an extreme of morbidity' (*WH* 13).

Through analysis he manages to reconstruct the story of her past and shed light on some of her symptoms. He discovers that Lisa's mother, who had died in a hotel fire, was not alone when she died, but had been having an illicit affair with Lisa's uncle. This induces two repressed childhood memories which centre on a sexual triangle of her mother, uncle and aunt. Exemplified by the figure of her mother, sex is inextricably linked to death in Lisa's unconscious: for her, as for Freud's real patient the 'Rat man', sexual activity brings on hallucinations of death. Freud is eventually led to a diagnosis, informed by his book *Beyond the Pleasure Principle* on which he is working at the time, which famously posits the existence of a 'death drive' opposing or complementing the 'pleasure principle', compelling us to endlessly repeat unpleasant experiences in order to master them and thereby choose our own path to an 'inorganic state', or death.[2] 'I began to see Frau Anna', he writes, 'not as a woman separated from the rest of us by her illness, but as someone in whom an hysteria exaggerated and highlighted a universal struggle between the life instinct and the death instinct' (*WH* 116–17).

31

This accounts for the first four sections of the novel, a generically promiscuous mix comprising a series of letters which serves as the Prologue, followed by Lisa's poem and journal, then Freud's case study, 'Frau Anna G.' The first half of the novel, in other words, confronts us with two different authors who each write different kinds of text. Lisa's work represents writing as hysterical symptom, expressing indirectly what its author cannot otherwise tell. The Freudian case study, in contrast, is a virtuoso performance of brilliant reasoning, backed up with a continued appeal to the authority of psychoanalytic theory. In the face of this formidable interpretative mechanism, Lisa quickly becomes ashamed of her writing and tries to disown it: 'the more convinced I grew that the "Gastein Journal" was a remarkably courageous document', Freud claims, 'the more ashamed Anna became of having written so disgusting a work' (WH 106).

The next half of the book, however, demonstrates that Freud's account is less authoritative than it seems. The fourth section, 'The Health Resort', is a portrayal of Lisa's life after analysis. It is now 1929 (the events in the entire novel can be dated accurately)[3] and Lisa is on another train journey, this time a real one from Vienna to Milan, where she is to play understudy to a renowned opera singer, Vera Serebryakova, who has been hurt. She gets to know Vera and her husband Victor Berenstein, a much older couple. Like her feelings towards her mother, her attitude toward Vera is ambivalent, and some of her hysterical symptoms return when she learns Vera is pregnant. She dreams of standing over a deep pit filled with coffins, Vera naked in front of her. About this time Lisa hears again from Freud, asking permission to publish her case study. She writes back informing him of details that she had held back from him in analysis (e.g. about her half-Jewishness, and about one of the primal childhood scenes, which it appears she has actually discussed at length with her aunt), and tactfully offering more plausible conclusions than some of his (e.g. about his rather forced opinion of her repressed homosexuality). Ominously we learn that she still suffers intermittently from the breathlessness and the pains in her breast and ovary. Her dreams about Vera take on a predictive quality in the winter of 1929 when Vera dies in childbirth. Five years later

Lisa marries Victor Berenstein and adopts his and Vera's son Kolya. For the first time in her life she has a fulfilling relationship, and suffers no hallucinations during intercourse.

Her marriage brings a fleeting sense of closure to the story which is immediately shattered by the terrible power of the fifth section of the novel, 'The Sleeping Carriage'. It takes place in September 1939, five years after Lisa's marriage. The brooding political climate glimpsed through Lisa's story in the previous section has now erupted into war. She and Kolya are living in a Jewish ghetto in Kiev, Victor having been murdered by the Stalinist authorities. Along with the other Kiev Jews they are rounded up, tricked into thinking they are being sent to Palestine, and brutally, cruelly murdered – forced to strip and watch the deaths of those before them in the queue, before being shot and pushed into the deep ravine. Though Lisa's gentile passport gives her a chance to escape, she stays to die with her son. But even in the pit her horror is not over. An SS guard realizes she is not dead, crashes his jackboot into her left breast and pelvis and rapes her with a bayonet. Her dying screams merge into those around her.

At this point the link between each of the sections of the novel is clear. The detailed focus on the horror of the Final Solution throws into question the sense that history is about progress, echoing the rhetoric of the opening of the novel, when the slow sea voyage in extreme fog undertaken by Freud, Ferenczi and Jung to spread the word of psychoanalysis to the New World of America is experienced by Jung as more like a journey 'back into the primeval past' (*WH* 9). It makes sense of Lisa's symptoms and makes clear why Freud, for all his interpretative gymnastics, is unable to explain them satisfactorily. Lisa suffers from a 'compulsion to predict' as much as she does a 'compulsion to repeat', and her symptoms relate to the impact of fate on a whole generation of Jews rather than a single individual.

It is not difficult to imagine why *The White Hotel* has proved so popular. It allows its readers to relive the darkest and most critical episode in our recent history from the perspective of the person with whom they have come to identify as the story progresses. Lisa is a kind of Everywoman, caught in the events at the very centre of the maelstrom that is twentieth-century history. The reader of *The White Hotel* comes to acknowledge while reading the novel – while, in other words, suspending disbelief – that the fiction is set alongside shocking events that really happened; it simultaneously refers to itself and beyond itself, an equivalent of that familiar cinematic device, 'based on a true story'. What we are presented with in Section 5 of the novel allows readers an accurate insight into the awfulness of the plight of real people like Dina Pronicheva. Furthermore, the novel's success can be explained by the fact that publication coincided with what historians and cultural theorists have documented as the flourishing of the 'Holocaust industry', a phenomenon born of our understandable need somehow to come to terms with the huge and terrible events which shaped our century, but which has become bound up with the workings of big business and mass media, rendering the Holocaust just another marketing phenomenon for the consumer to 'experience'.[4] Thomas has told of arriving in New York to promote his book and overhearing a radio advertisement urging listeners to 'experience *The White Hotel*' (LC 2). Promotional T-shirts produced by the publisher bore the legend 'I've stayed at the White Hotel'.[5]

But cultural appropriation of the Holocaust does not altogether account for the importance of *experience* in the reading of this novel. The way its form progressively opens out from subjective to objective narration demands from the reader a peculiar kind of emotional investment: we identify with Lisa, believe in her quest to be redeemed, and are then horrified as she is eliminated without warning. In an impressive reading of the novel, Rowland Wymer has argued that the cultural symbolism of fall and rebirth we all recognize (from the Bible and other myths and literary texts) is backed up at a psychic level, so that the equivalent of Paradise and Eden is the 'oceanic' space in which the child is united with mother.[6] *The White Hotel*, in other words, implicitly reinforces what it says explicitly, working on the reader at a conscious and unconscious level. And this also applies to what the novel says about authorship and authority. All along, whatever our misgivings about the power dynamics of psychoanalysis,[7] we invest in Freud's attempt to understand Lisa, to provide the authoritative account of her life story and neurosis, for we are engaged in a similar quest as we read the novel. Where Freud is ultimately frustrated, the reader comes to a shocking moment of recognition, as it becomes clear that Freud's authority is brutally destabilized by the inexorable movement of history.

It is crucial to the deconstructive effect of *The White Hotel* that this outcome has been foreshadowed all along by a continuous implicit questioning of Freud's voice. More extensively than Thomas's previous novels, *The White Hotel* weaves the voices of others deeply into its texture. According to Thomas, the novel was initially the product of a strange catalogue of predictive dreams, coincidental events and poems which seemed to come upon him from nowhere. More specifically, the process of conceiving and writing the first stages of the novel were the result of what he experienced as a kind of possession – more strange, more *telepathic*, than his possession by the spirit of Akhmatova in *The Flute-Player*. In the late 1970s, looking for a novel to read on a flight to America for a series of poetry readings, Thomas picked up Anatoli Kuznetsov's *Babi Yar*, the story of Dina Pronicheva's amazing survival of the massacre at Babi Yar in 1941. He was astonished by the parallels with a poem he had recently written, 'Woman to Sigmund Freud', but had put away in a drawer, unsure how to use it. Where his heroine had fantasized about a burned hotel, the Nazis had burned corpses; where skiiers were buried in an avalanche in the poem, Dina Pronicheva had feared being buried alive in the ravine; where the lake by the white hotel floods, so the Babi Yar ravine was later flooded after a dam burst its banks. Thomas concluded that the woman of his poem really '*was* Dina Pronicheva – or someone very like her' (*MH* 39–40). He cancelled the tour immediately and spent an 'obsessional day' planning a novel which began with a woman being treated by Freud for hysteria and ended at Babi Yar.

Lisa, then, is another example of the anima-heroine at the centre of each of Thomas's first two novels (both Jo and Elena prefigure her role as the 'neurotic as visionary'), and the first two chapters of *The White Hotel*, 'Don Giovanni' and 'The Gastein Journal', are effectively given over to the transcription of her voice. Artistic 'possession' was vital to the composition of the rest of the book, too. Realizing its keystone was to be a depiction of Freud, Thomas undertook an intensive programme of reading in order to acquaint himself with psychoanalytic theory and Freud's style. As a result, Freud seemed to speak to him. Although imitating the case study was a difficult process, 'Freud's voice, dry, remorseless and subtly erotic, carried me through. If the voice rang true, the chances were that I wasn't going too far astray, I hoped' (*MH* 47). Once the pastiche was complete, Thomas then sought 'an appropriate style' for the more conventional third-person narrative in the next section 'The Health Resort'. He imagined a text by 'a contemporary Turgenev, and translated it from his non-existent Russian' (*MH* 47).

This shows how readily Thomas turns to impersonation to overcome problems of composition. It also shows how he approached the most urgent difficulty – technical and moral – the novel presented him with, of moving satisfactorily from a subjective symbolist poem representing the world of the imagination to the objective detailed prose which would reflect collective historical experience. Having originally decided the novel must end at Babi Yar, it seemed natural to allow Dina Pronicheva, who had actually been there, to account for real historical experience by speaking once again through him (though this time filtered through another 'medium' as well, Kuznetsov):

> I felt that the only way I could do it would be to not play around with the Holocaust, but to accept the physical descriptions of the eye-witness, of Dina Pronicheva, as reported by Kuznetsov. Everything else could be and should be imagination and fiction at play – and of course there is a certain fiction, in that Lisa has a child and she has her own life – but I wanted her to become merged in the actual historical reality. So I dealt with the Holocaust in fiction by, at the last moment, letting history take over. (SL 73)

Thomas, in other words, felt he could only deal with the Holocaust in fiction by *refusing* to fictionalize it, or at least by minimizing the elements his imagination brought to the account – a strategy which, incidentally, is ironically close to the position of many of those who object to the novel on the grounds that the Holocaust cannot or should not be represented in fiction.

All this means that *The White Hotel*, as Patrick Swinden recognized, is founded upon a 'succession of imitations',[8] a series of meetings of authorial minds – not just Kuznetsov and Freud but also the woman of Thomas's poem or Dina Pronicheva, and his imaginary Turgenev. As such, it affirms Thomas's position as one of the foremost literary exemplars of Baudrillard's notion of simulation, the copying or reduplication of visual phenomena or systems of discourse so that the rational understanding of referentiality is lost. The effect of Thomas's simulation is contradictory. While he adopts the voices of Freud and Kuznetsov to stamp his text with authority, this very strategy also compromises the whole idea of authorized texts. This paradox is not entirely deliberate, however, as we can see from the Author's Note at the beginning – which is of course the first interpretation of the novel, even before it has begun. Using a characteristic metaphor, Thomas's note informs the readers that because the book is a journey into 'the landscape of hysteria' they will inevitably encounter the figure of Freud. Thomas is at pains to distinguish his 'imagined Freud' from the real one, emphasizing that while his version of Freud conforms to 'the generally known facts of the real Freud's life' and that he has 'sometimes quoted from his work and letters, *passim*', the role Freud plays in his novel 'is entirely fictional' and 'all the passages relating to psychoanalysis (including Part 3, which takes the literary form of a Freudian case history), have no factual basis'. Right away this preamble suggests that Thomas is struggling to retain control of the effects of his mimicry. Though it is true, strictly speaking, that the psychoanalysis of Lisa Erdman has 'no factual basis', the fiction is so cleverly inserted into fact that it subtly casts doubt on what we understand as fact.

Thomas's impersonation of Freud is the most extensive and *devious* act of mimicry in the novel, made up of a patchwork of quotations from Freudian cases, real letters, and technical papers like 'Analysis Terminable and Interminable' – a literary forgery so accurate in style and structure that, to the scholar of psychoanalysis, it is 'like discovering a lost Shakespeare play'.[9] It is a particularly effective example of the familiar metafictional practice of inserting a historical character into a novel and thereby blurring the ontological boundaries between fiction and reality, implying that what we know of the real Freud may be fiction.[10] But as well as doubling the fictional and the historical Freud, Thomas also combines two different 'real' Freuds. The letters at the start set the psychoanalytical context of *The White Hotel* as the period between 1909 and 1920, a crucial time for psychoanalysis, as it was undergoing a major shift from its earlier Oedipus-dominated incarnation, to one in which the 'death drive' became important, heralding Freud's later excursions into socio-historical psychoanalysis, as in *Civilisation and its Discontents* (1930). When Lisa comes to Freud, he has just written his paper on the uncanny (published in 1919), is working on *Beyond the Pleasure Principle* (1920) and will shortly write (at Bad Gastein in 1921) an article on telepathy (eventually published in 1941). But 'Frau Anna G.' is modelled on the work of an earlier Freud, one who had just revised his notorious 'seduction theory' and published similar short case studies in *Studies on Hysteria* (1895). One of these in particular, 'Elisabeth von R.', is the case on which Thomas based his simulated analysis, 'since it seemed to be about the right length and had an artistically satisfying form' (*MH* 47).[11] The trick Thomas pulls off in *The White Hotel*, then, is to tamper with psychoanalytical history so that this early Freud merges with the later one. 'Frau Anna G.' is similar in style to Freud's early case studies (including his famous ones, like 'Dora', 'Little Hans' and 'Ratman'), but also reflects a different Freud, who reads her case in the light of his growing interest in the death drive. Uncannily, the Freud we are presented with is familiar (his literary voice remains more or less the same, of course, throughout his work) and also made disturbingly unfamiliar too. The effect perhaps accounts for the fact that Freud's daughter Anna is said to have burst into the offices of the Freud Archives clutching a copy of *The White Hotel* and demanding, 'Where did he get these letters?' (*MH* 76).

In the Author's Note Thomas explains that he treats psychoanalysis as 'the great and beautiful modern myth . . . a poetic, dramatic expression of a hidden truth', but claims that 'in placing this emphasis, I do not intend to put into question the scientific validity of psychoanalysis'. But by doubling Freud as a poet or myth-maker the science is inevitably compromised. *The White Hotel* effectively foregrounds the three most controversial 'repressed' areas of Freudian theory, three 'unauthorized' departures from official Freudian doctrine which threaten to compromise the authorized theory: the death drive, which has long been the most contentious area of Freud's work among Freudians, Freud's notorious flirtations with the supernatural (represented in the novel by the reproduction (*WH* 175) of his extraordinary comment of 1921 that if he had his time over again he would devote it to the study of telepathy[12]) and, most disputed of all, the abandoned seduction theory.

Early in the history of psychoanalysis Freud began to realize that what he had taken to be patients' real childhood memories of being seduced by adults were in fact *fantasies* of seduction generated by Oedipal desire. While this development is only implied in *The White Hotel*, it is difficult to consider the novel's depiction of psychoanalysis without it coming to mind. Seduction is continually evoked, through references to the operas *Don Giovanni* and Tchaikovsky's *Eugene Onegin*, for example, and the many instances of seduction in Lisa's early life, like losing her virginity to a young soldier on a train. But the key 'seduction story' is psychoanalysis itself. What struck Thomas while researching Freud's case studies was that they were 'Viennese seduction stories. A troubled young woman came in and lay down on a couch; Freud, his cigar flaring, got to work on her, striving to strip her naked' (*MH* 46). As in seduction, Lisa and Freud take on precisely the roles each wants the other to be: his suggestions shaping her statements and behaviour ('And now you mention it, I suppose my brother comes into the dream', *WH*, 96), her awareness of psychoanalytic theory leading him on to his interpretations ('I've just sung in a new oratorio called Oedipus Rex – can you tell?! I like the idea of clarification', *WH* 178). Eventually, just as he mistook fantasies for recollections of real events in the early years of psychoanalysis, Freud is unable to distinguish between Lisa's reminiscences and her premonitions.

Baudrillard has argued that Freud's difficulty with the seduction theory highlights the fact that the very object of study in psychoanalysis, the unconscious, is a model of *simulation*, something that continually generates signs and symbols which bear no relation to reality and yet which also *affect* – perhaps even constitute – the subject's experience of reality. This is apparent above all in hysteria, a condition in which *real* symptoms emerge from *imaginary* or unreal conflicts.[13] Though Lisa is closer to the ancient figure of the hysteric as clairvoyant (SL 83) than Freud's later, psychopathological version, and though her symptoms are produced by real future events rather than past ones, Lisa is still a hysteric in Freudian terms in the sense that her body conveys in coded form precisely what she is unable to express directly. Her symptoms lead Freud on to the wrong diagnosis. In this sense *The White Hotel* supports Baudrillard's conclusion that psychoanalysis is dominated by a logic of seduction rather than interpretation, as it demonstrates how, in the course of his investigations, the psychoanalyst is seduced into thinking he is uncovering the truth when in fact he only encounters a reproduction of the psychoanalytic edifice itself reflected in the mirror-like surface of the symptom. Freud sees in the object of study only what he wants to see – or what Lisa wants him to see – not what is actually *there*.

Throughout, then, at a deep level, *The White Hotel* continually undermines psychoanalysis. That it does so while also conveying Thomas's obvious admiration for Freud, however, suggests that what the novel really seeks to challenge is the idea of 'authorized' reading itself. As the Freudian reading of what happens in the novel collapses, 'unauthorized' readings are opened up. One of these, as I have outlined, is a Baudrillardian one. Another is suggested by Linda Hutcheon, who discusses the novel as if it is an exposition through fiction of the staple tenets of poststructuralist theory.[14] But the most powerful alternative reading is implied in the novel itself.

Carl Jung is a shadowy presence throughout, given his role in the Prologue. There he interprets one of Freud's dreams about his sister-in-law Minna so persistently, clearly suspecting it reveals something about Freud's private life, that Freud is annoyed and refuses to 'risk his authority' by discussing it further. Jung tells Ferenczi that at that moment he felt 'Freud had *lost* his authority, as far as he was concerned' (WH 11). This implies that a quite different analysis of Lisa is possible if we appeal to the authority of Jung. Where Freud saw all symptoms as pointing backward to an originary trauma, Jung held that they can also look forward to a point at which the psyche will be more balanced; the unconscious tries to 'compensate' for what is lacking or unbearable in the conscious mind. Psychopathology, in other words, could be anticipatory as well as retroactive – a contentious notion, as it counteracts the conventional understanding of causality.[15] Jung placed a special emphasis on dreams in this regard, reaffirming the traditional assumption that they were predictive rather than produced by the past. A Jungian reading of *The White Hotel* would have no difficulty accommodating the fact that Lisa's symptoms are future- not past-directed. This reading is even more convincing if we consider the striking parallel between Lisa's condition and the episode in Jung's own life, in 1913, when he began to experience vivid dreams, hallucinations, visions of drowned bodies and seas of blood. Fearing at first a lapse into psychosis, he then 'realized' that his symptoms were in fact caused by an unconscious apprehension of the First World War.[16] Even more remarkable are the similarities Rowland Wymer has traced between Lisa's story and the real-life case of Sabina Spielrein, a Russian Jew who was a patient of first Freud and then Jung, suffering from either mild schizophrenia or severe hysteria, who was shot by the Nazis in 1941.[17] She is now credited as being one of the key figures in effecting Jung's break from Freud, contributing to his thinking on the reconciliation of oppositions, the importance of looking forward to death, and the function of the anima.[18] One of Jung's most successful challenges to the authority of Freudian theory was his view that many people diagnosed as hysteric were probably mildly schizophrenic, since both conditions were rooted in a split personality. Thomas has said he was unaware of Sabina Spielrein while writing *The White Hotel*;[19] it is tempting to imagine how different the novel might otherwise have been. It is also tempting to speculate what would have happened if Lisa Erdman had gone to Jung rather than Freud.

The Jungian reading of the novel has a certain authorized quality, given the importance of Jung in Thomas's approach to literary creation. Yet what we might regard as Thomas's 'own' reading of the novel is in fact even more readily available, again in the novel itself. For *The White Hotel* does not end at Babi Yar. Feeling he needed to 're-assert the life principle' after the horrors of 'The Sleeping Carriage' Thomas composed a final chapter, a 'spiritual fantasy' to match the sexual fantasy of Lisa's poem and journal, and 'Freud's fantasy of who she is' (SL 87). Called 'The Camp', this section is a vision of the 'after-life' – not necessarily one that accords with religious belief, but the only characters who appear are those whom we know are dead. Lisa is there, Freud is there, and his dead daughter and grandson. Vera Berenstein sings on the radio. Finally, Lisa encounters her own mother. This has proved the most puzzling section of the novel, and can be interpreted in many ways: as proof of the final triumph of the imagination over history, an ironic comment on narrative closure, a dramatization of what we might 'dream of' after death. Some critics find the 'glib "sunshine after tears" atmosphere' after such a harrowing depiction of the Holocaust offensive.[20] There has been disagreement about where exactly this camp is supposed to be: heaven? A fantasy version of Palestine? Thomas himself has described it as a version of (Dante's) Purgatory, more appropriate for Lisa than Palestine as she is brought up a Catholic rather than a Jew, and, unlike heaven, 'painful but with a kind of purity and a purpose and a quest' (SL 88). What is most significant is that this is the only section – apart from the very end of 'The Sleeping Carriage' which leads into it, and the Author's Note – which is not a simulacrum of a previous author's voice. It is thus more than just an add-on, a way of removing the bitter taste of Babi Yar, but a conclusion which represents everything that has gone before.

On first reading it seems that its title, 'The Camp', should have been swapped with the title of the previous chapter, 'The Sleeping Carriage'. But it is true to the symbolic logic of the novel that each chapter is almost interchangeable: one is a public, historical account of death, the other is a personal account of death. The afterlife is presented as a kind of inverse concentration camp, where different nationalities respect each other, where the dead are systematically brought to life, via the same bureaucratic mechanisms of files and papers used by the SS to put the living to death. The dead are transported to the promised land in trains, just as the condemned are taken to their deaths. Instead of death, however, the experience is described as 'emigration' (*WH* 234). This indicates that a densely worked 'symbolic economy' operates in *The White Hotel*, in which all of its key signs are interchangeable. The resorts and hotels are equivalent to the death camp, trains are both a literal and metaphorical means of passage, a fantasy and real space. The peat-bog graves mentioned by Jung at the beginning become the mass grave at the end, the emerald lake beside the white hotel becomes the stagnant lake which Babi Yar turned into once the Russians flooded it after the war. This network of equivalence was precisely what Thomas planned: 'Ideally I hoped someone could open the book anywhere and read a paragraph and it would make them think of some other episode in the book, some other particular image' (DW 34). The same is true of the central concepts the novel explores: sex is equal to death (Eros v. Thanatos) and vice versa, history is equal to myth, fiction to reality. Public history impacts on private psychic history. Time works backwards as well as forwards, cause is determined by effect.

The novel works, in other words, just like the unconscious, generating an economy of signs which lead, as Baudrillard says, to seduction rather than interpretation. Freud defined the unconscious as a realm in which separate impulses, even those which seem mutually contradictory, can coexist naturally side by side. In the unconscious there is 'no reference to time at all', no reference to reality, all events are potentially present at the same time.[21] Ultimately this is true of *The White Hotel*. It continually disrupts linearity, merges or sets against one another different systems or entities. Each meaning, each reading, is placed under the influence of an alternative. This process is exemplified, above all, by its central symbol, the opaque and suggestive white hotel itself. Freud sees it as the mother's body (*WH* 105); Thomas himself thinks it symbolizes 'life, [which] was made for pleasure and happiness; but there was something in its very fabric which demanded self-destruction' (*MH* 40); Hans Sachs, most satisfactorily perhaps, reads it as a version of 'Eden before the Fall – not that love and death did not happen there, but there was no time in which they could have a meaning' (*WH* 14–15). But it could just as easily figure as death itself, or the afterlife, the health resort or the camp.

That everything in the novel is equivalent or reversible applies at the level of structure too. *The White Hotel* works, appropriately enough, given the significance of opera in the novel,[22] like music, expressing itself through harmonies and contrasts between the different sections and voices. Its seven parts are each separate, self-contained entities, different generically, which refuse to comment directly on each other. They simply exist side by side, like the unconnected juxtaposition of sentences linguists call 'parataxis'. The novel's effect comes from association, as the reader relates the different sections to each other as s/he reads. The resulting symbolic excess might account for its success, why many readers experience *The White Hotel* as something 'more' than a book.[23] But it also explains why seeking an authoritative reading of the novel is simultaneously so seductive to both readers and critics alike and so often unable to capture its essence.

Perhaps the last word on the subject should go to its author. In his contribution to the *TLS* plagiarism debate, Thomas (speaking in his own voice) addressed the capacity of the novel to seduce people into discussing other matters than the novel itself and concluded that what the debate came down to in the end was that there were those who liked the novel and those who did not.[24] Both within its pages and in the academic debate about the novel, *The White Hotel* represents the triumph of artistic expression over critical interpretation.

4

Acting Out: The *Russian Nights* Quintet

Coming after a novel as overtly psychoanalytic as *The White Hotel*, the *Russian Nights* sequence can be seen in Freudian terms as a five-novel attempt to 'work through' the issues raised, both public and professional, by the phenomenon of its predecessor. Most troubling was the alarming crisis in identity Thomas experienced as a result of his sudden success. As he put it in the *New York Times* article he wrote to explain his flight from Washington: 'I found myself walking around, or teaching, in a bell-jar. I was a "celebrity"; my words sounded pompous and hollow to me. I'm sure it was my own fault, but I began to lose touch with who I am. I was, to everyone, "the author of *The White Hotel*", so I began to see myself in the same light' (LC 4). Reference is made throughout the quintet to the critical furore which surrounded *The White Hotel*, in particular to acts of blinkered interpretation and to the popular conception of a successful novelist. In *Sphinx* there is talk of 'an English writer who had struck it lucky with a shrewd mixture of sex and violence' (*Sph* 146). In *Ararat* one writer, Victor Surkov, defends another who has been accused of plagiarism: 'I don't think Sholokov plagiarized. But of course he, in a way, didn't write it all alone ... Merely because all art is a collaboration, a translation if you like. But plagiarism is a different matter' (*A* 141).

Such references suggest that *Russian Nights* is an extensive course of fiction as self-analysis. But they also point to its function as a sustained inquiry into Thomas's art. Despite the planning and research they required, the previous three novels had been composed more or less intuitively. Thomas's appropriation of the various authorial voices in *The White Hotel* was essentially instinctive. *Russian Nights* is much more self-conscious and deliberate. Yet for a writer who feels that 'life and art [are] too close, like *Titanic* and ice-berg' (*MH* 136), this kind of bold journey into the creative self has its dangers, and perhaps it is no coincidence that Thomas was to end up in real therapy before the sequence was finished.

The quintet is organized around the idea of improvisation, 'the mysterious way in which a word, an image, a dream, a story, calls up another, connected yet independent' (Author's Note to *Swallow*). The novels are each made up of a series of stories improvised by a number of recurring characters. The central figure is that of the *improvisatore* (or its female equivalent the *improvisatrici*), the curious blend of artist and actor whose vocation neatly encapsulates the tension between originality and borrowing which is central to Thomas's aesthetic. The *improvisatore* must follow the directions he is given, but is free to make something new out of them. In one obvious sense, then, this central conceit enables Thomas to include in the quintet many examples of his characteristic form of literary impersonation, 'doubling' Pushkin in *Ararat*, H. Rider Haggard in *Swallow*, and Freud in *Lying Together*. But in doing so it allows him to pursue more doggedly the implications of his conviction that literature is, as his character Surkov says, a matter of collaboration and translation, developing out of ideas and images 'planted' in the author from other people or chance events outside. *Russian Nights* spells out what Thomas's previous novels imply, that improvisation is not a subdivision of art but the activity on which all art is founded.

The uncanny implications of this fact are explored in the quintet, too, most strikingly in the character of another Russian poet, Sergei Rozanov. When improvising, his face and voice change dramatically according to who is narrating. It is most alarming to those who witness it, even to Rozanov himself on one occasion (in *Lying Together*) when he suddenly finds himself reproducing Freud's voice, speaking in perfect German, even though he claims to know none. Rozanov's improvisations are often described by another metaphor which underlines the mystical side of artistic endeavour, that of shamanism, the 'primitive practice of self-denial so that one could travel in the land of the dead and return unscathed' (*LT* 11). This clearly appeals to Thomas's Jungian sensibility. Ventriloquism allows him to journey in the land of the dead we know as literary history, negating his own authorial identity and voice to become an other.

Improvisation, however, is just one of the elements which unite the chaotic mass of stories in *Russian Nights*. The quintet builds on *The Flute-Player*'s concern with Russia, and its status as a crystallized version of the relationship between modern history and the subject, especially the artist. Russia was a muted presence in *The White Hotel*, of course, figuring as the Berensteins' homeland, and the place where Lisa's tragic fate is determined, but the quintet explores Thomas's interest in Russia head-on. For a sequence primarily about the blurring of fiction and reality, Russia has an obvious attraction. As one character asks in *Sphinx*, 'where could one find a more fictional reality, or a more all-too-real fiction, than in Russia?' (*Sph* 90). Though Russian politics and society are frequently depicted and discussed by the characters of the quintet, it is the artistic side of Russia which is most central to *Russian Nights*, more so even than to *The Flute-Player*. Where that novel was inspired by Akhmatova, *Russian Nights* (as the Preface to *Sphinx* declares) is dedicated to Pushkin.

Surprisingly, for an author who had already translated Akhmatova, Thomas discovered Pushkin belatedly, as a result of being at a loose end after the closure of Hereford College in 1978, where he had taught for 14 years, and returning to Oxford to begin a BLitt on 'Problems in Translating Pushkin'. The thesis was never finished, but Thomas took from it an enduring fascination with the writer. As with Akhmatova, Pushkin's value to Thomas extends beyond the literary. Where Akhmatova figures as Thomas's muse, Pushkin stands as his historical alter ego. It is clear from his introduction to *The Bronze Horseman*, his translation of his poetry, that Thomas is attracted by Pushkin's personality – his polemicism and nonconformism, his liking for scandal, his superstitious nature. What is more, Pushkin seemed to see the twentieth century coming, in all its horror and magnitude. His 1833 poem 'The Bronze Horseman', which Thomas regards as his masterpiece, 'encompasses the essential story of the next century and a half: the hapless struggle of the individual to survive, in an increasingly estranged urban environment, against absolute power – whether of emperor or ideology'.[1] This quality connects to his ability to anticipate the psychological realism of later European works. Pushkin serves as the supreme literary model for Thomas, the key to his realization 'rather stupidly late in life . . . that I could write a different kind of novel'.[2] Pushkin was famously experimental, writing, often simultaneously, in a huge array of literary forms (both poetry and prose) and modes (realistic and fantastic). His originality paradoxically owed a great deal to his skill as an adapter of previously existing forms and ideas, founding the entire Russian literary tradition by borrowing – translating – from the established German, French and English traditions 'imported' into Russia: 'All that he read and heard he transformed into his own uniquely balanced harmonious style'.[3] Equally attractive to Thomas was the fact that such formal innovations were less the fruit of a systematically realized aesthetic vision than the product of a restless creative spirit. Pushkin's tendency to leave works as fragments because he felt he had said enough to make them perfect appealed to Thomas: 'I loved the way he would break off abruptly, as if to say, That's it! I'm bored! It's enough!' (*MH* 55). In other words, Pushkin shared Thomas's fondness for stylistic promiscuity, moving 'obsessively from one work to another' as he 'moved from woman to woman'.[4] The example he set enabled Thomas to achieve his aim to find an 'inclusive form' for *Russian Nights*, 'one that would allow me to switch easily from fantasy to reality and back, from fiction to poetry to drama to autobiography – anything I felt like' (*MH* 136).

Pushkin's role as catalyst to the quintet goes deeper still. Where the *improvisatore*, according to tradition, extemporizes on a subject suggested by the audience, *Russian Nights* is developed by Thomas from a theme suggested by Pushkin. Its 'major source of inspiration' (according to the Preface to *Sphinx*) is *Egyptian Nights*, Pushkin's unfinished story about the mysteries of improvisation. It tells the story of the poet Charsky who is visited by a strange Italian *improvisatore* asking him to help him become known in Petersburg society. To test him, Charsky invites him to improvise on an ironic theme – the poet's own right to choose his subject. He is so astonished by the *improvisatore*'s extraordinary gift that he secures an invitation for him to improvise at the Princess's Palace. There the title he is given for his composition is 'Cleopatra and Her Lovers', a subject that recalls one of the precursors of Pushkin's story, *Arabian Nights*. Cleopatra offers herself to any man for a night who is ready to pay the price with his life at dawn. The story is left tantalizingly unfinished. Thomas has said that he was fascinated by the way the story 'moves from prose to verse, from the present to the past, from realism – tinged with the uncanny – to myth ... I liked the blurring of boundaries, in form and atmosphere', not to mention its concern with 'Eros and Thanatos again' (*MH* 56). This description, of course, has echoes of Thomas's own fiction, and it is clear from the numerous references to *Egyptian Nights* Thomas has made in interviews and elsewhere[5] that the story has been internalized by him as the embodiment of his own art. Most obviously the story's metafictional treatment of improvisation raises the question of where a work of art – and indeed its author – begins and ends. How original can any work of art be? How far can any author retain control of its meaning or effects?

The centrepiece of Thomas's first novel in the series, *Ararat* – which was originally titled *Improvisatore* (DW 37) – is a reproduction of *Egyptian Nights*, translated by Thomas, which he then continues and completes. For much of the book, in other words, Thomas becomes Pushkin in the way that he becomes Freud in *The White Hotel*. But to add to the complexity, neither translation nor completion is presented straightforwardly, under Thomas's own name, as it were, but is embedded within a complex arrangement of narratives nested inside one another which narrative theorists call the 'Chinese-box structure' (though a more appropriate metaphor in this case would be a stack of Russian dolls) which sets the pattern for the quintet as a whole. The continuation of *Egyptian Nights* is supposedly the work of Victor Surkov, a Russian poet who seems in a sense to be the reincarnation of Pushkin, combining a vulgar heart with an effortless creative brilliance. But Surkov himself is the invention of Sergei Rozanov, who, at the beginning of the novel, improvises a story to amuse himself and a blind woman he has ill-advisedly chosen to spend the night with. Surkov writes his *Egyptian Nights* while on a nightmarish sea voyage to the United States – but this eventually turns out to be an anxiety dream he has while on a real journey by plane to the United States.

Surkov takes up Pushkin's story by having the *improvisatore's* performance of 'Cleopatra and her Lovers' so well received that eventually it is translated and published by none other than Pushkin himself. Pushkin thus curiously makes an appearance in what was originally his own story, and the resulting unnatural union of the worlds of historical reality and fiction seems to lead directly to catastrophe. The *improvisatore's* recital has enraged one of the listeners, who misreads in it a personal insult and challenges the Italian to a duel. Arriving at the location for the duel, Charsky and the *improvisatore* find that an earlier duel has just taken place at the same spot. The loser was Pushkin, who has been killed – as he really was, in 1837 – by his brother-in-law d'Anthès. Surkov is alarmed at the way his fiction has run out of control and taken on a life of its own. He concludes that his improvisation is somehow to blame for Pushkin's death: if it hadn't developed in the way it did, Pushkin would not have fought. Surkov hastily rewrites the ending, this time ensuring Pushkin is sent away out of harm's reach by the authorities for publishing scurrilous verse, and sacrificing the *improvisatore* instead. The effect of this revision is to show how the artist can reassert his privileged role as ultimate controller of his text, no matter how removed from its genesis and development he may have been. Pushkin is allowed to survive and history is thus altered. But this outcome in turn leads to an even more troubling sequence of events. The *improvisatore* dies, but not in the duel. When he arrives at the scene where it should take place, he finds himself 'looking down at the field of history, where the revolt of the Decembrists was about to be mounted and crushed' (*A* 120). Two armies face each other across the square. The *improvisatore* walks into their midst and is killed accidentally by an officer intending to give him a warning. As in *The White Hotel*, there is at this point a sudden intervention of the vast force of history impinging on the lives of defenceless individuals.

This heralds one of the key concerns in *Russian Nights*, and which is constantly returned to in Thomas's works (particularly those of the nineties): the complex relationship between freedom and determinism in art and history. Art is presented as an uncanny force, its own strange logic of causality making it impact on the real world, affecting and anticipating history. On the other hand, history is envisaged as a paradoxically unalterable structure which shapes art and which art is powerless to affect. This explains the title of the novel. Mount Ararat is in Armenia, the setting for one of the most ominous yet forgotten events in twentieth-century history (which was prefigured by the Decembrists riot in 1837 and which also anticipated the Jewish holocaust), the brutal and systematic attempt by the Turks in 1915 to wipe out an entire race of Armenians, a subject referred to in the novel. But it is also the biblical location where Noah's Ark came to rest. Like the image of the white hotel, Ararat simultaneously stands for the fateful world of contemporary history and a world beyond history, a pastoral haven where peace and tranquility reign and which promises resolution and regeneration.

Ararat was envisaged as a single novel until its final page, when, Thomas says, 'it seemed to open out; and seemed also to invite me, the author, into the fiction' (*MH* 135). Only then did he realize another volume was required. This indicates that as well as being about improvisation, the form of *Russian Nights* is itself improvisational. The characteristic Author's Notes which begin each novel tell a shorthand story of how the sequence loosely took shape: *Swallow* is called the second in a 'sequence of improvisational novels', by *Sphinx* it has become a four-volume series, in *Summit* it has a title, *The Russian Quartet*. But after four novels 'the characters still haunted me and the theme just wouldn't let me go'. *Lying Together* duly appeared, giving the sequence its title *Russian Nights*, finally freeing Thomas 'like an animal releasing its prey'.[6]

The eponymous image in *Swallow*, the novel which *Ararat* leads into, stands for improvisation itself. Its central character, the *improvisatrici* Corinna Riznich, compares improvisation to 'a swallow's flight; like leaping from stone to stone across a river in flood – the excitement and danger of not daring to miss your footing or else jumping onto a stone leading nowhere'

(*Sw* 232). This is how Thomas imagines that writing works: flitting from one idea to the next, crossing the boundaries of fiction and reality, text and author. *Swallow* is about a fictitious storytelling Olympiad at Lake Lemminjärvi in Finland (inspired partly by an open-air writers' conference in Finland to which Thomas was invited in 1983, partly by the laurel crown for which the great female Italian improvisatrici competed throughout the nineteenth century) and consists of representations of the contestants' entries interspersed with the machinations of the judging process. This device enables Thomas to create an immediate 'twist' in the story of *Ararat*: that entire novel is revealed to have been Corinna's entry in the Olympiad. *Ararat* has thus been 'swallowed' by the next novel in the sequence, causing us retrospectively to revise our reading of it.

Ararat is in fact never referred to in *Swallow* by that name. Its 'real' title is *The Seven Veils*, a reference to the story of Salome, who so transfixed King Herod with her erotic dance (removing veils one at a time, a forerunner of striptease) that he gave her the head of John the Baptist – a story which has clear parallels with the central triangle of sex, death and storytelling at the heart of both *Arabian Nights* and *Egyptian Nights*. Indeed we can understand *Russian Nights* as embodying Barthes's conclusion to his famous reading of Balzac's 'Sarrasine' that desire in narrative operates as a kind of 'economic system' whereby stories are traded for something desired, such as a night of love, a body, or survival: 'one does not narrate to "amuse" or "instruct" . . . one narrates in order to obtain by exchanging, and it is this exchange that is represented in the narrative itself.'[7] What we have in *Swallow* is a series of narratives which operate as acts of seduction, in the manner of 'Sarrasine' or *Arabian Nights*. The reader is led on, transfixed like the watcher of striptease, the exposure of each narrative frame like the erotic promise of a veil being lifted to reveal the object of desire . . . only for another to appear beneath. It is a link Thomas had made before in a poem which refers to Salome, 'Poetry and Striptease' (from *Dreaming in Bronze*), in which a writhing girl becomes 'only a medium for what her nakedness/ still veiled' (lines 31–2).[8]

The image suggests that *Swallow* shifts the emphasis in *Russian Nights* from the process of writing to the act of reading.

The sheer number of different stories which are inserted into each other in the novel (reminiscent of Italo Calvino's *If On a Winter's Night a Traveller*, 1981) seduce the reader into trying to order all its segments into one coherent master narrative. But the narrative framing is so complex, and the frames so frequently broken, that this becomes almost impossible, or, more importantly, pointless. The function of the repeated framebreaking is to divert our attention away from the content of each story onto the very mechanism itself. The point of reading *Swallow*, in other words, is not to determine which narrative or narrator is more 'real' than any other, and which story most 'true', but to recognize what the novel tells us about the seductive process of literary creation and reception.

Swallow is more playful than *Ararat*. This is clear from one of its stories, a 'scandalous amendment' (Author's Note) of Haggard's *King Solomon's Mines*, where the English adventurers, driven to delirium by their experiences, begin to swear violently at each other, sink into sexual degeneracy, and even eat the natives who carry their baggage. The parody is part of a magazine article supposedly written by an English *improvisatore*, Southerland, which turns out to be another version of Thomas's 'primal' autobiographical story, his puberty in Australia (central to which was the erotic charge he experienced from the journey up 'Queen Sheba's Breasts', Mount Ararat in Haggard's romance).[9] The article is reproduced in the novel as evidence in the judges' case against Southerland for plagiarism in his poem *White Nights*. This kind of self-reference by Thomas piles on the layers of irony in the quintet, reinforcing its concern with the multiple identities involved in authorship. The insertion of the autobiographical extract into *Swallow* raises the stakes in the metafictional game played by *Russian Nights*. Because it is part of a work of fiction – that is, surrounded by clearly fictional narratives – it raises the question of whether the author's memories detailed in the account are fictionalized or genuine, or even whether he himself can be sure. What is certain, though, is that it is the most effective piece of narrative in the novel, hilarious and affecting by turns. As such it emphasizes the weakness of some of the other stories. *Swallow* often seems less the product of Thomas's desire to extend the novel form than an opportunity for his restless imagination to flit swallow-like from one interest to another in whichever form he pleases.

The third novel in *Russian Nights*, *Sphinx*, is less convoluted in form and far darker. It is a kind of literary *troika*, driven by exercises in the three major literary forms, drama, prose and verse. It opens, though, with a short verse Prologue (composed in the classic 'Pushkin' stanza form), part overture, part coda to the two previous novels in the quintet, mentioning images and themes from each. As the only section of the novel whose narrator is unidentifiable (it could plausibly be Thomas, Pushkin, or any of his other alter egos from the first two novels), it reminds us of the quintet's interest in the metaphorical process of collaboration involved in authorship. This is accompanied, in the rest of *Sphinx*, by a concern with collaboration in its more sinister, political sense. 'Love Train', for example, the second section, tells of a prudish Welsh journalist, Lloyd George (who is not, as he embarrassingly has to repeat, the famous British prime minister), who becomes infatuated with an actress he encounters on a trip to Russia, Nadia Sakulin, who, however, turns out to be a 'swallow' (the Russian name for a seductress-spy) looking to secure her defection to San Francisco by framing him. But the key section is the first, an expressionist play called *Isadora's Scarf*, influenced by the stylized theatre of avant-garde Russian director Vsevolod Meyerhold, who appears in it in dreamlike interludes.

Isadora's Scarf was originally commissioned by the BBC as a television play but was revised for the novel. It tells a rather melodramatic tale in which Rozanov just avoids being murdered when his mistress's lover mistakenly kills his near-namesake, the poet Gleb Rezanov. Both are obsessed by the fatal web of connections which began with Isadora Duncan, the pioneer of modern ballet, whose 'dancing celebrated the glorious freedom ushered in by the October Revolution' (*Sph* 32), and whose scarf 'binds together the whole glorious history of our epoch' (*Sph* 33). Duncan suffered a horrific death in 1927 when her luxurious long red scarf caught in the spokes of the wheel of her convertible, breaking her neck. According to Rozanov the scarf then became the property of her husband, the notorious Russian poet Sergei Yesenin, who shot himself in

1925, wrote a farewell poem in his own blood, and hanged himself with the scarf. Next it passed to his ex-wife Zinaida Raikh, who was then married to Meyerhold. Shortly after being released by Stalinist authorities she was brutally murdered – still wearing the scarf – by a mysterious intruder into her apartment. The scarf then passed to Meyerhold himself, who was wearing it when he was shot by the KGB. Just before his murder Gleb Rezanov tells Rozanov that he knows how Zinaida was killed and is himself in possession of the scarf.

Whether the scarf *was* actually present at these events cannot be proved, but what is more important is that it symbolizes the mysterious process of cause and effect in history. If Rozanov can discover who Zinaida's murderer was and what the motive was, he feels certain 'we would have solved the enigma of life itself, of Russia, the sphinx' (*Sph* 25). This impossible task relates to Thomas's motivation in writing the novel. Its central image came to him while on a plane journey over Australia when he was suddenly struck by the powerful sense that 'time and the world are an illusion'. Looking down on the Pacific, over which he travelled years before on the way to Melbourne, he wonders if his 14-year-old self is still *there* somehow, on the deck of the boat, waiting for an ice-cream. At that age, 'the world was inside me, I could grow it as I pleased; now – if there is a now – it is outside me and I am helpless to change it'. 'Now' means after the Berlin Wall, after Vietnam, the Kennedys, Aids: 'What *improvisatore*, I wondered, had spun that narrative, and why? The curving glittering ocean turned to me the face of a sphinx, and a new novel stirred in me. And my own infinitesimal life – the sphinx had shaped that too'. The sphinx, in other words, is the mysterious web of temporality and causality which makes things what they are. It is 'murk itself, the sphinxes of love and history, smiling at our pathetic attempts to clarify them with left- or right-wing values and ideologies' (*MH* 114).

Given the labyrinthine connections evoked by this central image, it is not surprising that Thomas found *Sphinx* by far the most difficult part of the quintet to write. It meant attempting to grapple with the sublime, that which is unrepresentable because unthinkable. His difficulty is perhaps most visible in 'Luibov', the final section. It is a poem (again in the Pushkin stanza pattern) written by Rozanov, who is now in a *psikhushka* (a mental asylum), on request of his psychiatrist, Luibov. Ostensibly, then, its function is therapy, but it is really an elaborate coda to the earlier sections of the novel. The stories of Lloyd George, Rozanov himself, and others, are all continued and the symbolic texture builds up to a bewildering crescendo of references to the key motifs and images of the three novels in the sequence so far (sphinxes, swallows, the scarf, 'puberty's white nights', etc.) and a dramatization of the last days of Pushkin's life, when he is feverishly attempting to complete *Egyptian Nights*. Looking back on the novel, Thomas thought he had tried to put too much in, lacking 'the calm and the skill to fine it down' (*MH* 134). The symbolic overburdening of *Sphinx* suggests that Thomas's concern with his own art was turning disturbingly into a crisis in identity played out in the novel.

The next novel in the sequence, *Summit*, is certainly much less intense. As a compressed work of satire it is a departure from the *Russian Nights* template. Thomas claims in the Author's Note to 'have followed an ancient tradition in which a serious trilogy is succeeded by a farcical or satirical coda'. True to the logic of the other texts, though, its place in the elaborate set of Russian dolls the sequence had become by this stage is clarified in the opening chapter. Nadia Sukulin is involved in a plane crash as she escapes to America after framing Lloyd George. Before the plane starts to nosedive, she had been reading part of a novel called *Swallow* (which she didn't much like) in which Victor Surkov meets President Tiger O'Reilly. *Summit* appears to be her 'death-dream', continuing this story by telling of a farcical summit meeting between O'Reilly and the Soviet leader, Grobichov. Both are thinly veiled caricatures of who proved to be the last world leaders of the Cold War, Ronald Reagan and Mikhail Gorbachev. Their encounters are full of comic misunderstandings which actually cause them to like each other and jettison the entourage of assistants and advisers who surround them anxiously, preferring to meet with their wives and talk on their own. The result is an upturn in the fortunes of O'Reilly's public persona, as his confused remarks in interviews are regarded by some as bringing a welcome new honesty to politics, and a warming of the relationship between the two superpowers.

Summit's satirical impulse switches the focus in the quintet from improvisation to artifice, and a concern in particular with the way political discourse works to disguise the way things really are from the people. Thomas's abilities as a mimic are well suited to parodying the idioms of political discourse – the presidential addresses, the machiavellian behind-the-scenes dialogue of the advisers and apparatchiks, the blunt way major statesmen might actually speak to each other. However, the satirical edge is not sharp enough: the portrayal of the two leaders struggles to go any deeper than contemporary newspaper sketches of Reagan and Gorbachev: O'Reilly borders dangerously on the insane, Grobichov is sharp-witted, randy, but cultured. More effective as political satire is a brief moment when Thomas moves back onto the territory he has made his own. *Summit* reintroduces one of *Ararat*'s most memorable characters, the odious war criminal Finn, a man 'as old as the century' (*Sum* 12) who wandered around the boat Surkov dreamed he was on in that novel telling anyone who would listen about his role in the worst atrocities of the century, like Babi Yar and Armenia. By now he has received the Nobel Peace Prize, and, to rapturous applause, gives a speech detailing how he has 'served the cause of peace' throughout the century, helping to 'ease the overcrowding' in the death camps at Auschwitz and Dachau, helping alleviate the Armenian problem in Turkey and the Jewish problem in Europe. He poses as a man of principle, an idealist, modest at his success because 'there is still so much work to be done. There are thousands of people alive today who have never looked with terror down the barrel of a gun . . .' (*Sum* 15). The exaggerated logic of reversal is blackly comic, but powerfully evokes the rhetoric used by political régimes to justify a course of action.

Writing later, Thomas gave a more revealing explanation for the appearance of *Summit*, admitting that he had 'forced himself' to write something that could bring the quartet (as it then was) to a close, even though he knew it was 'crude, over-the-top stuff' (*MH* 165). By this stage his faith in the project was waning. In his memoir he calls the sequence 'laboriously evolved', likening himself at the time of *Summit* to 'a frenzied *improvisatore* on a stage, gabbling into the darkness'

(*MH* 165). The hint of madness in this description is not accidental. After writing *Summit* Thomas fell into an extreme depression during which he was unable to write or even read for a year. As he explains it in his memoir, this had much to do with the final collapse of his first marriage and the physical effects of serious illness, but the existential demands of composing a self-analytical sequence like *Russian Nights* doubtless exacerbated his condition. Part of the problem, he has said, was 'the danger of writing, the perilous closeness of fact and fiction, and the proximity of the edge'.[10] What lifted him out of his block were two experiences of confession: entering psychoanalysis for the first time, and writing his memoir.

Memories and Hallucinations, sandwiched between the last two volumes of *Russian Nights*, is an astonishingly frank autobiography, a portrayal so honest in some respects (such as Thomas's discussions of his sexual history) that it is a wonder he did not lapse into depression again. One reviewer called it 'an extraordinary public masturbation of the darker side of his mind'.[11] But as starkly honest as it is, the message of the memoir is that identity, like art, is a kind of improvisation which blurs the distinction between fiction and reality. The point is made by its title, an echo of Jung's autobiography, *Memories, Dreams and Reflections*. No attempt is made to clarify which episodes recounted in the book are memories, and which hallucinations. The memoir's non-linear structure reflects 'the waywardness, the apparent randomness of memory' (*MH* 191), leaving the reader without a sense of definite chronology in which to place the episodes which are recounted. Both memory and hallucination problematize our relationship to reality: it is uncertain whether memories reflect the 'true course' of events in any person's life or are distorted by the framework of remembering, and hallucinations, by definition, have only limited basis in the real world.

The memoir's emphasis on the confusion between what is real and what is fictional is not simply the product of its author's playful desire to keep the reader guessing about his true identity. It opens with Thomas's admission that he is frightened by 'the coincidences that seem to cluster around art' (*MH* 2), and tells repeatedly of occasions when he has experienced a strange overlapping of art and life – such as when he unwittingly had Freud quote in *The White Hotel* precisely the same lines from Goethe as the real Freud used in accepting the Goethe Prize for Literature in 1930, or when a neighbouring Jewish Centre caught fire during a reading of the novel (*MH* 76). He reveals that for years he kept a 'journal of coincidences' (like Jo in *Birthstone* (*B* 24)) only to find he had so many entries that he had to conclude that 'coincidences are no coincidence' (*MH* 10). The point is that literature is something that continually breaks down the boundaries between reality and fantasy in a more disturbing way than the deployment of self-reflexive strategies within its pages. Art itself is uncanny, in the Freudian sense, dealing in repetition and mystery, making the familiar unfamiliar.

According to Freud, the uncanny returns us to an ancient *animistic* sensibility, in which there is no distinction between the real world and the world of the mind.[12] This is a good description of the world of Thomas's fiction as a whole, and *Russian Nights* in particular. We can find many instances in the sequence that are governed by an animistic logic: when Surkov is frightened when his extension of *Egyptian Nights* unaccountably leads to death in the Decembrists revolt, or when Nadia Sakulin reconstructs a complex chain of events that supposedly proves that 'Rezanov was murdered, and Rozanov is enduring a living death, because I performed in a play by Chekhov!' (*Sph* 171). It explains the many references to chaos theory, in which chance and determinism are blended together (e.g. *Sph* 67). Most of all, the metaphors of improvisation and shamanism reflect the uncanny process in authorship by which thoughts and moods are projected from one self to another and the division between the real world and the world of the mind is broken down. Thomas has spoken of the relevance of the Jungian notion of 'synchronicity' to his experience of writing. He envisages

> related ideas and coincidence as some kind of almost physical law ... a grid of relationships, of which metaphor in writing is an example. Everything relates to everything. It's a mesh. And then there are extraordinary coincidences – usually trivial things – but they're like mountain tops peeping out of the sea. They're just an indication of the range of relationships that lie under the surface. (DW 42)

This description also works as a summary of how to read Thomas's novels and the symbolic economy that operates within them – and which intensifies throughout *Russian Nights*, when, as each successive volume appears, a new set of symbols is made available. The uncanny world of animism, as Freud says, is preserved in neurosis as well as art, and it is not surprising that inhabiting art too intensively should endanger the health of the author.

The last novel in *Russian Nights*, *Lying Together*, is written on the wave of autobiographical honesty started by *Memories and Hallucinations*. Thomas 'himself' features in the text so prominently that it is as much a kind of sequel to the memoir as a conclusion to *Russian Nights*. Though he has never been far from the surface during the quintet, he has never been a central character, never come face to face with the people he has created. As Surkov tells him, while his own life has been laid bare in the sequence, Thomas himself has got off lightly: 'A few memories of your adolescence, in *Swallow*, was pretty safe territory' (*LT* 30). *Lying Together* redresses the balance, enabling Thomas to take *Russian Nights*'s concern with improvisation and collaboration to its logical conclusion and thus provide an appropriate end to the quintet. It tells the story of how 'Thomas' and his characters Rozanov, Surkov and Masha Barash, who have all featured previously in the sequence, meet at a fictitious conference for writers in London in 1988, where they produce a series of improvisations to occupy themselves in the evenings – all 'lying together', as Rozanov quips (and, this being Thomas, the phrase applies in its other sense too). In the now standard *Russian Nights* fashion, the reader is plunged into the fictional worlds created by the collaborators, each of whom takes it in turns to narrate, picking up where the previous tale left off. 'Thomas' plays to the gallery, choosing a typical piece of literary impersonation: a fictional correspondence between the notorious Austrian sex psychologist Richard von Krafft-Ebing and one of his enlightened readers, a young masochistic servant girl Sophie Arendt, which is reminiscent of the seductive relationship between Freud and Lisa in *The White Hotel*. The different contributions are punctuated by the story of the relationships between the four writers.

There is a certain tension among the group. It transpires that the previous volumes in *Russian Nights* were the results of a collective effort (*Summit*, for example, is here revealed to have been a collaboration between Thomas and Masha Barash) but the Soviet régime's persecutory attitude to art meant that each had to appear solely under Thomas's name. Now, after *glasnost*, they feel it is time for them to receive their due credit. Surkov includes some of the improvised material from the novel at his reading at the conference to make sure 'Thomas' acknowledges the collaborative nature of the work or else has to face charges of plagiarism (*LT* 180). Thomas is depicted, in other words, with no small degree of irony, as a figure who arouses suspicion, an impostor. Towards the end of the novel, the authors discuss the finished form of the novel their improvisations will constitute, and decide that 'Thomas' is to be the narrator. He wonders 'what parody of my voice they would create, and would it be any less "true" to me than the voice I might have created for myself? Probably not: for after a few decades of life wasn't everyone – driven by forces beyond his control – semi-fictional at best?' (*LT* 233).

Thomas carries the central conceit as far as he can. In the Author's Note he acknowledges 'the collaborative assistance throughout of my Soviet friends Sergei Rozanov, Victor Surkov and Masha Barash'. Appearing on this page, conventionally an 'extratextual' section of a work of fiction, where we can take it that the author speaks the truth, this credit gives readers a jolt. Can it really be the case that characters who had seemed previously to be the creations of other characters in the sequence are real? Having the author descend onto the same ontological level as the rest of his characters is a common practice in works of metafiction, and results in a characteristic double effect: while making the characters seem as real as the author, it also implies that people in the real world are no more than fictional constructions. Here *Lying Together* underlines the principal message of *Memories and Hallucinations* (the only difference being that one conforms to a genre associated with reality and the other to one connected with artifice): any presentation of self is unreal, improvised. 'Thomas' tells Masha in *Lying Together* about his memoir: 'A lot of that book is fictional. You know how it is, Masha. We live fictional lives' (*LT* 103).

But the gesture of sharing the credit for the novel with three fictitious characters can be read on another metaphorical level, too: Rozanov, Surkov, Barash – also Pushkin, Haggard, Krafft-Ebing – *are* collaborators in Thomas's work. To put it romantically, they are his alter egos, his muses. But, in theoretical terms, they represent the complex mixture of those internalized voices of the authors who have influenced him and the different discourses which exist in his unconscious. 'Only gradually', 'Thomas' says of his co-writers, 'was I learning to adjust; learning to take some pleasure in their twofold existence – in their own consciousness and between the covers of novels bearing my name, somewhat inaccurately, as author' (*LT* 29). This admission is thoroughly Bakhtinian in its awareness that the author's word is no more than equivalent to any of the other voices which inhabit his text – it does not reign supreme, but is equal. Of Rozanov and Surkov, Thomas says that when he first met them 'six or seven years ago, they made a big impression on me. As honest and honourable Russian writers, they seemed to me to be emblematic in some way. I couldn't have got the same effect if I'd fictionalized them' (*LT* 107). As the statement implies, they are of course fake, but real as well: both are emblems – or Jungian archetypes – in Thomas's restless creative mind.

5

Dreamtime: *Flying in to Love* and *Pictures at an Exhibition*

With its direct self-portrait, *Lying Together* brings *Russian Nights* to a close and also effects a kind of 'end of analysis' as far as the quintet's function as self-inquiry is concerned. The work that comes after is less self-conscious, seemingly more at ease with itself formally. Thomas is nothing if not an obsessional novelist, however, and the most important novels in the period from 1992 to 2000 continue with the major preoccupations in his fiction, especially the way the nightmarish events of the twentieth century intersect with and produce the tissue of fictions and fantasies within those who live through it.

Flying in to Love and *Pictures at an Exhibition*, the two novels which came after *Russian Nights* each focus on one of the key traumatic episodes of recent history – the assassination of John F. Kennedy in 1963, and the Nazi genocide, respectively – moments which, like trauma in the individual psyche, help shape the very fabric of late twentieth-century Western consciousness while remaining visible only through their representations, proving impossible to assimilate satisfactorily into cultural knowledge. The traumatic quality is clearest in the case of the Kennedy assassination as its effects were intensified by the increased power of media technology at the time; it is summed up by the cliché that everyone can remember what they were doing when Kennedy was shot. We know what Thomas was doing when Kennedy was shot because he has told us – groping a hairdresser 'when that tremor went/ across the screen that's still not stopped –/ Kennedy shot' ('Big Deaths, Little Deaths', lines 4–6). It is worth remembering one obvious reason for Thomas's deep interest in these historical traumas (though not obvious to some of those who accuse him of exploitation): like many others, he has 'lived' through them. While he had little direct contact with the Second World War (his father was too old to fight, and his home town the target of only one serious bombing), he remembers being aware of the horrible events being played out distantly on the historical stage: 'In newspapers and newsreels I see the dead and the living skeletons of Belsen. Not even a sheltered Cornish boy can see such images without being changed forever' (*MH* 72). But what makes his novels about each of these episodes particularly powerful is that, like *The White Hotel*, they place the 'nightmare of history', as Thomas summarizes that novel (*MH* 44), centre stage rather than leaving it to figure, as it does in *Russian Nights*, as a haunting presence behind the more central concern with art.

Flying in to Love begins with a strange, disembodied narrative voice, and the effect is immediately more unsettling than the direct addresses of *Lying Together*:

> 'Ten thousand dreams a night', a Dallas psychologist told me, when I dined with her and her black lover, 'are dreamt about Kennedy's assassination.' Since dreams begin anywhere, and since fiction is a kind of dream, and history is a kind of dream, and this is both, we could begin with the shots in Dealey Plaza; or, a few seconds and an eternity later, the screaming cars and motor cycles through the triple underpass, the nightmare of blood and brain, heading not for the Trade Mart but Parkland Hospital, so conveniently near by. (*FL* 3)

The novel is less complex in structure than any of Thomas's novels since *The Flute-Player*, but this unidentifiable voice suggests that beneath the apparent formal unity are a number of characteristic traversals of formal boundaries. By the end of the paragraph we are into the story, and in the mind of the first character. We thus move from Prologue into main story without warning, not even a change of paragraph. The 'I' of the first sentence never returns, though it is later implied that this is Thomas 'himself' speaking. The Dallas psychologist appears as a character in the book and reports a meeting with 'a British author who interviewed me during his writing of a book about Kennedy' and tells her that he had always dimly associated Kennedy with his father but only realized this twenty-five years later after a dream. This is 'why he had never been able to accept that Kennedy was dead' (*FL* 195). In this way Thomas writes himself into the novel just as surely as he does in *Lying Together*, though much more subtly, and in a way that highlights an author's uncanny ability to move between the boundaries of narrator and character. The opening thus complements the novel's concern with the distinction between personal and public history. Where does one end and the other begin? Fiction and history, it suggests, are indeed like dreams, in that they have an internal logic and system of signification which elude us, and are not best understood through conventional approaches to time and causality: all time is potentially present. Contemporary experience, *Flying in to Love* affirms, is more of a dream or a poem than a coherent narrative.

The novel comprises two main narratives. The first tells the story of the assassination through the experience of the main players in the drama (Kennedy himself, Jackie Kennedy, Lee Harvey Oswald, his wife Marina, president elect Lyndon Baines Johnson), while the second features a group of teachers and pupils from the Sacred Heart Convent School in Dallas who were supposedly among the last to meet Kennedy on his fatal route, all of whom have been deeply affected throughout their lives by their experience. Characteristically, Thomas opts not to tell the story in linear fashion, but shifts between past and present, between recollections and hallucinations in the minds of the central characters. Kennedy comes across as a modern Don Juan, his mind filled with memories and fantasies of sexual rather than political conquests. Jackie reads her book of symbols, regarding the gift of red roses at the airport as ominous, wondering about the strange man with the umbrella who appears during the motorcade.

Of the invented characters, two are especially central. Sister Agnes has spent the decades since the murder obsessed with Kennedy, making the assassination part of the school curriculum, and spending her spare time editing a journal about the assassination called *November 22*. The trauma of that date brought on a profound crisis in her faith in both Catholicism and history, each of which revolved around the desire to find meaning and coherence in the universe. With Kennedy's death 'she had, in a way, entered history, herself, and the shock had been enormous. History was what happened to you ... and it made no sense' (FL 165). By contrast, her colleague Sister Beatrice writes academic articles which read the assassination like a literary text, tracing the symmetrical motifs and subplots in the story. So persuasive is the evidence of intricate design that she wonders, 'who can now imagine as we did at the time – except in rare moments – that John F. Kennedy's assassination in Dealey Plaza was avoidable? No author could have hit upon such a complex pattern on the spur of the moment' (FL 55).

The novel, then, details two main approaches to understanding history: it can be read as either purely the product of chance, or as a predetermined plot. As such, Flying in to Love is an example of what Linda Hutcheon has termed 'historiographic metafiction', fiction which deconstructs the ideology that a narrative in history is simply 'found' by the historiographer and faithfully reproduced, by demonstrating that instead it is plotted, constructed after the event, subject to the same laws of selection and design as fiction.[1] The Kennedy assassination illustrates this idea particularly effectively, of course. Our knowledge of it as a historical event is practically inseparable from the mass of conspiracy theories which surround it, which testify to the problems involved in representation and interpretation. The conspiracy theories are part of Flying in to Love, but Thomas is less interested in solving the mystery or explaining precisely how the conspiracy unfolds than he is in exploring the assassination's seemingly endless ability to generate conspiracy theories. This means that, although Flying in to Love is an example of historiographic metafiction, we might say it focuses on the *phenomenology* of the crisis in historiography rather than the clash between signifying practices. It thus manifests the 'neurotic' logic evident in Sphinx and Memories and Hallucinations (the logic upon which conspiracy theory is also founded) where chance events are perceived as elements in a preordained pattern.

Like neurosis, the world of Flying in to Love is an animistic one where the effects of the assassination collapse the boundaries between mind and external reality. This leads to the novel's most important interpretation of the assassination, voiced by Jane Pulman, the psychologist of the opening chapter, who is one of Agnes's former pupils. Precisely because the conspiracy theories are so inconclusive, she thinks, the assassination must be seen as myth, as something which is unbelievable yet expresses a deeper truth. For many people, she writes,

> the assassination occupies a kind of dreamtime. Kennedy is dead, he is not dead. He is being taken back for burial at Arlington; he is flying on to Austin. A physicist said to me that those few seconds carried too great a burden of event, of shock, and it was as if that weight caused time to cave in, creating a vortex, a whirlwind, in which past, present, and future, and reality and illusion, became confused. (FL 195)

Parts of the story of *Flying in to Love* take place, in fact, in this mythic 'dreamtime', depicting a parallel universe where Kennedy survived and he and Jackie continue with their visit to Texas (an expression, perhaps, of Thomas's self-confessed inability to accept that Kennedy died).

Pulman's theory also explains the title of the novel. Its significance is obvious in that Love Field was the name of the Dallas airport where the Kennedys touched down on their fateful trip. From Sister Agnes's religious point of view, too, the end of Kennedy's journey was 'heaven or purgatory' (*FL* 123). But, in Thomas's writing, of course, love figures as the equivalent of death, and *Flying in to Love* similarly revolves around his preoccupation with Eros and Thanatos. Three times in the novel the same exchange occurs, like a repeated motif in a dream: Governor Connally's wife turns to Kennedy and beams: 'Mr President, you can't say Dallas doesn't love you!' to which he replies 'I sure can't' (*FL* 160). Pulman thinks that America loved Kennedy in such a violent ambivalent way because he embodied so many of its fears and desires (figuring as ultimate hero, villain, womanizer, etc.), that it had to kill him: 'The assassination was the *Liebestod*, the ultimate penetrative orgasm. He got really fucked. With all our violence and anger – Vietnam and other liberation movements, including the drug culture and feminism – it is quite obvious the myth for our time had to be a man's exploding head' (*FL* 193). The potency of this myth is conveyed most directly on the two separate occasions a character (firstly the seedy David Ferrie, and then, most outrageously – so outrageous in fact that it suggests Thomas is indulging in a little self-parody – Sister Beatrice) is brought to orgasm by imagining the fatal shot to the head (*FL* 18, 70). Like the white hotel and Mount Ararat, Love Field is a symbolic location where Eros and Thanatos, and the religious world of purgatory and the psychic world of the unconscious, are combined. Jane Pulman explains Kennedy's womanizing in conventional psychoanalytic terms as a restless yearning to return to the 'Love Field' of his childhood union with his mother (*FL* 196). She thinks the back pain from which Kennedy suffered throughout his adult life was a symptom of this desire. It also – like Lisa's precise physical symptoms in *The White Hotel* – foreshadows the sniper's bullet that will hit him beneath his shoulder blade (*FL* 259). Kennedy himself dreamily connects Love Field with the churchyard Johnson has told him about where he wishes to be buried (*FL* 207). As he is shot, Kennedy wants to get there, and feels as if he is flying, already part of his own myth.

While writing *Flying in to Love*, Thomas was also working on another novel. *Pictures at an Exhibition* began as a story of 'contemporary people undergoing psychoanalysis' and evolved, 'painfully, slowly',[2] to become Thomas's second book which extensively confronts psychoanalysis with the Holocaust. The opening section is one of the most powerful and affecting pieces of prose he has written. It tells the story of the friendship that develops between Bertold Lorenz, an SS doctor, and Chaim Galewski, a Czech Jew who has managed to secure his survival in the camp by assisting the doctors in their work. Lorenz is suffering from severe headaches and horrible nightmares, and has asked Galewski to try and treat him using psychoanalysis.

The opening section revolves around a serious of evening meetings between the two in Lorenz's house, conducted as secretly as possible, for it is not in Lorenz's interests to be seen to be playing host either to neurotic symptoms or a Jewish science. The comfort of his house is a stark contrast to the abjection all around it. There Galewski listens to opera and eats Frau Lorenz's delicious cooking. The environment confirms the impression of Lorenz as a serious, cultured and indeed *humane* person, even despite his frequent outbursts of vicious anti-semitism. He is disappointed when he hears the news that his sister has been caught stealing food from the grocery shop where she works, when 'none of his family had ever been caught in a criminal act before' (*PE* 47). Disturbingly, the novel demonstrates how in the midst of an apparent breakdown in civilization, the niceties of social convention – serving coffee and cake, listening to Mozart, quoting from the Bible – continue rather than cease. Their work is discussed by the two men as if they are in a quiet university science laboratory rather than a death camp. This ironic contrast is enhanced by Galewski's voice, which narrates: calm, measured, intimate, drawing the reader immediately in to an instantly realistic fictional world, reminiscent of Turgenev or – more appropriately, given this author's status as a key reference in the novel – Kafka's 'A Country Doctor'. Though the chilling undercurrents never allow it to develop into full comedy, a black irony underlies the basic premise. At one point Lorenz suddenly exclaims, sweat pouring from his brow, '*Why do I always dream of death . . . Why do I always dream of death?*' (*PE* 36). Galewski replies he doesn't know, unable or unwilling to make the link between being implicated daily in everyday scenes of the utmost brutality and the onset of severe neurotic symptoms.

The main part of the novel moves the action into contemporary London, focusing on a community of characters – friends, analysts, analysands – grouped around the dying psychoanalyst Oscar Jacobson. Jacobson is a wise authoritative figure, loved to some degree by them all, who nonetheless borders on the despotic, not unlike the mature Freud. Though we are never told explicitly, we suspect that he is an older version of one of the characters in the opening section. The problem, though, is that it is never clear which one. He could plausibly be an older version of Chaim Galewski, for a move into psychoanalysis proper would be a plausible post-war career after his experience of Auschwitz (and his obvious wealth and distinguished status would seem poetically justified rewards for his ingenuity and suffering). But he could just as easily be Lorenz, who also became interested in psychoanalysis through his encounter with it in the camp.

Jacobson possesses a carved wooden likeness of his own head, just like the one Dr Lorenz had in his study in Auschwitz, and has named his holiday home 'Padernice', the Nazi euphemism – signifying a non-Jewish heaven – for the destination of the trains taking Jews to their death. The confusion is increased rather than dispelled with the appearance later of a Dr Becker, a fit and healthy man, though not much younger than Jacobson, who claims to have been an officer in the Wehrmacht who worked with Dr Jacobson treating refugees after the war 'at one of the camps' and has since been living in Syria. As Becker introduces himself to the others, the terminally ill Oscar mumbles 'enem – friends', which is quickly interpreted by Oscar's wife Myra as 'We weren't enemies but friends' (*PE* 149–50).

The mystery is impossible to unravel, and this accounts for the novel's heightened suspense, and also its repetition of *Flying in to Love*'s rhetoric about the ultimate impenetrability of historical truth. But the real power of the novel comes from the implication that the two men embarked on a certain course at Auschwitz that brought them closer and closer together until they are indistinguishable. In the Auschwitz sections they grow to resemble each other as they grow to like each other, each being partly persuaded by the other's worldview. Though a victim, Galewski is also a collaborator, helping the SS men to prepare lists of people to be sent to their death, and is the subject of much hatred and even an assassination attempt from his fellow prisoners. Lorenz confesses to Galewski that one of his grandfathers was Jewish (*PE* 257), and tells him, 'I feel closer to you than almost anybody' (*PE* 255).

The idea of doubling is continually suggested in the novel: Lorenz has two sons, Hitler and Kafka are described as 'one person split in two' (*PE* 228), and there are references to the hideous experiments with twins conducted by Joseph Mengele (one of the historical referents for the book, being one of the real Auschwitz doctors who is believed by some to be still alive). In fact, the very idea of the 'Auschwitz doctor', whose business was to simultaneously end and preserve life, suggests the meeting of opposites. It was a job made possible, Robert Jay Lifton has suggested, through a psychological process of 'doubling', splitting the self into two parts in order to do the hideous work which would have been at odds with the normal ethical responsibilities of the doctor.[3] Like *The White Hotel*, then, *Pictures at an Exhibition* is governed by an overall sense of reversal – in the end, aggressor and victim, psychoanalysis and Nazism, love and death are as close together as they are distinct. Each character, concept and image in the novel *collaborates*. This applies especially to Thomas's twin obsessions, love and death. Like most of his other novels, *Pictures at an Exhibition* grew out of an image rather than an idea or character. This time, however, it was another's image – Norwegian expressionist painter Edvard Munch's *Madonna*, a representation of a young woman who seems simultaneously alive and dead. Seven of the novel's nine sections (which work contiguously, like *The White Hotel*) are named after works by Munch (hence the novel's title).[4] But perhaps the key work evoked by the novel is Munch's *Death and the Maiden*, the picture which gives the first section its title.[5] It depicts a naked vampiric woman, bold and unafraid, locked in an erotic embrace with a blackened skeletal figure who represents death. It is thus well suited for the dark mixture of eroticism and death in the Auschwitz section of the novel, and is specifically echoed when Galewski and his lover Judith join their skeletal figures in lovemaking while the screams of burning victims sound nearby (*PE* 259). Most appropriately, the painting seems to depict a victory for neither Love nor Death but a mutual desire for and – as the woman's attitude undeniably suggests – uncomplaining *acceptance* of one another.

Given its emotive subject matter, it is not surprising that the familiar charges of sensationalism and opportunism were made against Thomas on publication of the novel. The case was most forcefully stated by Bryan Cheyette in a review of the novel in the *Times Literary Supplement* which accused him of engaging in 'historical revisionism', failing to preserve Auschwitz as 'a source of unknowable horror' and making it instead 'a source of redemptive sado-erotic metaphors'.[6] The book is not immune to attack, for the third section's reproduction of documentary material from a book called *Those Were the Days: The Holocaust Through the Eyes of the Perpetrators and Bystanders* (acknowledged in the Note at the beginning), no doubt intended to provide the novel with the stamp of historical authenticity, does seem a little too tangentially related to the rest of the book, never as satisfactorily integrated as *Babi Yar* in *The White Hotel*. Yet behind Cheyette's argument is precisely the assumption the novel challenges, the implication that the Holocaust has nothing to do with – and should be kept separate from – art, metaphor, or the discursive patterns of history.

To begin with, it is actually not true to say that Auschwitz is 'unknowable' – impossible for those living in another time to experience the exact nature of its horrors, perhaps, but not unknowable. Countless photographs and documents – like *Those Were the Days* – exist to prove otherwise (one only has to consider the wealth of material available on the Internet). Thomas's novel is disturbing because it dares to confront the questions that many would rather not face, about what Hannah Arendt famously described as the 'banality of evil',[7] or the fact that the appropriation of art was crucial to maintaining the ideology which seduced otherwise 'normal' people to collude or take part in a psychopathic programme of mass murder. In Auschwitz in particular, embodied in the horrific opera-loving figure of Mengele, murder was continually eroticized and aestheticized. The numerous references to Central European art in the novel – Mozart, Goethe, Mahler, Kafka, etc. – underline the fact that the people who perpetrated the atrocities were, on the face of it, capable of great cultural discernment. Lorenz tells Galewski how the planners of Buchenwald were careful to build around Goethe's favourite oaktree (*PE* 22) and recalls references to Homer in one of Hitler's speeches (*PE* 27). This is what is really disturbing about the events in Central Europe during the war: it is all too easy to disown the Nazis by labelling them as evil, but in important respects they were just like us. Instead of accusing Thomas of arrogantly remaking Auschwitz 'in his own image', one could argue that his novel focuses – deliberately, provocatively, and not without its problems, it is true – on the aspects of the death camp which are most disturbing of all to those of us interested in the power of art and myth.

Similarly, it is not necessarily a negative judgement to suggest that the Holocaust figures as a myth in our culture, though that is generally the tone of those, like Baudrillard or Peter Novick, who argue that it does. As Jane Pulman's reading of the Kennedy assassination suggests, myth is not just a negative term connoting untruth, but a valuable way in which a culture can come to terms with and articulate its history and identity. In fact, as Daniel Schwarz has suggested, this might account for the growing number of literary explorations of the Holocaust which, like *The White Hotel*, employ fantastic or symbolic modes.[8]

In *Pictures at an Exhibition* the link between art and the Holocaust is central to the novel's concern with the complex way the public external world impacts on the private internal world. Oscar's wife Myra (the only present-day character to admit to being at Auschwitz) tries to cope with the pain of her past through painting pictures inspired by the Holocaust, and Chris James, one of Jacobson's trainee analysts, writes a thriller called *Patterns of an Observed Disturbance*, based on speculation about Jacobson and Myra. Edvard Munch's paintings have no direct link to the events in the novel (though he was labelled 'degenerate' by the Nazis, and was treated after his breakdown in 1908 by a Dr Jacobson), but they figure as examples of the foreshadowing so central to Thomas's work. A comparison is made between Munch's characteristic spectral figures and the physical effects on the prisoners in the death camps. Galewski frequently comments on their skeletal features in a way that calls to mind Munch's most famous painting, *The Scream*. (Munch's accompanying comment, 'I felt a scream pass through nature', is reproduced in the novel.) The mysterious Becker describes this painting as 'a prediction of the twentieth century. It's a very realistic portrayal. We saw many like that in the refugee camps, your therapist and I. Stick-people, no longer human. [...] And those men in long coats – well, I've seen them many, many times. Gestapo' (*PE* 155).

6

Doubling Thomas: *Eating Pavlova* and *Charlotte*

Though they deal with typical Thomas preoccupations *Flying in to Love* and *Pictures at an Exhibition* are unusual in that they contain no deliberate parody or incorporation of another author's voice. The books acknowledged at the start of *Flying in to Love* were 'consulted for background information and speculation' only and *Those Were the Days*, *Pictures at an Exhibition*'s equivalent of Kuznetsov's text in *The White Hotel*, is reproduced verbatim, without being altered or framed. In contrast, Thomas's next two major novels, *Eating Pavlova* and *Charlotte*, are both sustained impersonations of other authors. Though the former was acclaimed by reviewers and the latter roundly condemned, the responses generally acknowledged that each was the kind of novel only D. M. Thomas would attempt or could pull off. One review of *Eating Pavlova* saw the introduction of a new word: 'Thomasine'.[1]

As if to emphasize its concern with merging authorial identities, *Eating Pavlova* begins, characteristically, with a credit to a previous text. This time, though, it is one of Thomas's own. *Eating Pavlova* started life as Chapter 11 of *Lying Together*, where Sergei Rozanov improvises, in a shamanic trance, a monologue delivered by the dying Freud in his garden in Hampstead. Thomas includes this in the new novel and picks up where he left off, producing a work which displays his extraordinary technique of literary ventriloquism at its most ambitious and sustained. Where *The White Hotel* gives us the public voice of Freud, an uncannily accurate impersonation patched together from real Freudian texts, here we have the

74

private, inner voice of Freud, one that we never – or perhaps seldom – encounter in his published work.

Eating Pavlova is a memoir supposedly written by Freud in 1938–9, the last year of his life, when he had fled Nazi Vienna and settled in Hampstead. There, suffering appallingly from the pain of his cancerous jaw, visited and written to by a number of contemporary VIPs and nursed by his dutiful daughter Anna and his personal physician Max Schur (who had both agreed to Freud's request to end his life when he asked), Freud lived out his last year in as much comfort as his deteriorating condition could allow. In his memoir Freud gives accounts of his dreams and key elements from his life in a state of morphine-induced near delirium. This gives Thomas ample opportunity to write in a dreamlike, richly associative 'Freudian' style. Often it is unclear – Freud is unsure himself – when he is dreaming and when he is remembering. Voices suddenly seem to speak within his head. He comes to realize that accessing the truth of the past through historiography is only equivalent to the hazy truth of memory or even hallucination. This is why the book contains no acknowledgements to any specific Freudian texts, even though it sticks closely to the framework of Freud's known life and includes quotations from and allusions to some of the most autobiographical of his theoretical works.[2] *Eating Pavlova* is a Freudian fantasy, a version of history which closely follows the established course, but which is altered in the way a dream disfigures reality.

The title conforms to Thomas's usual practice of naming his novel after a central organizing image, which offers a way in to the symbolic and conceptual core of the book. Early on, Freud alludes to a dream of the nineteen-month-old Anna (*EP* 17) discussed by the real Freud in *The Interpretation of Dreams.*[3] Deprived of food all day because of a stomach upset due to eating too many strawberries Anna calls out for 'stwawbew-wies, wild stwawbewwies' – an unconscious retaliation, Freud thought, against the restrictions imposed by authority. To-wards the end of the novel, Freud has a dream which is the inversion of Anna's, featuring a huge well-stocked delica-tessen, in which Anna is the only person who refuses to help herself to anything she wishes except some 'stwawbewwies' which are positioned beside a Pavlova. As he interprets it, while all around her 'mankind is sating its libido without reference to morals or other inhibitions', Anna remains disciplined and ascetic. This leads him to consider his own sense – part regretful, part proud – that he has refrained from gorging on the pleasures life had to offer because of his devotion to his family and to psychoanalysis. This points to the dream's real value, as 'the very incarnation of the dreaming process. In our conscious life we have to ask for everything via the shop manager or assistant. [. . .] Whereas in the unconscious we just throw everything into the vast trolley of the libido' (*EP* 255).

'Eating Pavlova', then, is a byword for satisfying the desires of the libido, and the novel is mainly about Freud's secret satisfactions and frustrations in his hidden erotic life. *Eating Pavlova* clarifies some of the many opaque areas that remain in Freud's biography despite the minute scrutiny of his life by biographers – in particular his relationship with the three key women in his life: Martha his wife, Minna Bernays her sister, and Anna. At the centre of the novel is a complex *ménage-à-trois* involving Freud, Martha and their neighbour Philipp Bauer. As Thomas's Freud anticipates, Bauer does feature in biographies of him, but only in a limited capacity, as the father of one of his most famous patients, Ida Bauer, known to posterity as 'Dora'. The story of their relationship suggests why Freud was so unable to preserve a position of impartiality in her case, for Bauer effectively traded his daughter for Freud's wife, handing her over to him for his work and receiving Martha in return. The intrigue draws in the young Anna, too, attracted by the air of sexual duplicity. We are provided with an extract from a pornographic fantasy the young Anna herself has written, called *Strictly Private*, in which she fictionalizes the story of her parents' renewed love for each other once Bauer has ignited Martha's sexual desire, and which demonstrates (proving speculation) that her feelings for her father – and vice versa – threaten to go beyond a telepathic empathy. Most significantly, we learn that Freud and his sister-in-law Minna did indeed sleep together on occasion, as some biographers have suspected, though their relationship was far from a conventional illicit affair. Rather Freud initiates an elaborate game of deception – a version of the Cyrano de Bergerac story – whereby he encourages Minna to write uninhibited letters to his notorious confidant Wilhelm Fliess, confessing her sexual frustrations and desires. He then poses as Fliess and writes seductive replies, urging her to confide in Freud and perhaps even use him to relieve her frustrations physically (which she duly does).

This story foregrounds the key 'Thomasine' motifs of doubling and forgery. Freud stands in for Fliess just as Thomas stands in for Freud in the novel. And Freud is also aware of how his masquerade can influence reality and alter history. He imagines the furore caused by the discovery of his forged letters to Minna, how scholars will struggle to relate these to the letters he wrote Freud; in these new ones Fliess 'will gain immense and undeserved credit for his superb style and his brilliant flashes of psychoanalytical insight. They will say, Freud stole shamelessly from Fliess' (*EP* 65). But once again Thomas's aim is more than simply to underline the problems of gaining a suitable foothold in acts of historical interpretation. Thomas doubles Freud again, but this time he does so by effectively doubling himself. Here we have Freud depicted as cultural *provocateur* (not unlike Pushkin), stubbornly publishing his last major work, *Moses and Monotheism*, a text designed to enrage the Jews at the most sensitive time in Jewish history, against the advice of almost everyone. We have Freud the seducer – not a Don Juan, who seduces directly, but a brilliant manipulator of language, capable of fooling and seducing anyone. Most of all, we have the Freud only hinted at in *The White Hotel*: a mystical, more poetic double whose understanding of the symbolizing potential of the human mind explodes into the poetic stream-of-consciousness which constitutes *Eating Pavlova*'s narrative style, in which everything is capable of referring to everything else. Freud's mind is perceived (not implausibly) as a mass of tumultuous connections and associations, verging on the interpretative endeavours of paranoia.[4] He admits, for example, that while writing *The Interpretation of Dreams* he lived

in a creative trance like a poet; at times I was sunk in paralysis and depression. I was plunging into my own underworld. I should make it clear that no paralysis, depression, castration complex, matricidal or patricidal urge, hysteria, neurasthenia, sexual perversion, suffered by any of my patients could begin to rival the equivalent mental state or perverse desire in my own psyche. (*EP* 58).

Recast as a poet in Thomas's own mould, Freud is of course presented as a figure deeply in tune with the supernatural elements of life. This is also quite plausible, as Freud's superstitious nature, his fascination with telepathy and numerology is well known. But the novel gives us so many examples of precognition and synchronicity that he seems at times more like Jung. Such examples become more common as the novel moves towards the end. Freud remembers noting in his 1915 diary (snatches of which are reproduced in the novel) that he feels troubled by the 'overwhelming hysteria' of Vienna during the war: 'Mostly women, of course: full of tics and writhings and compulsions of one sort or another. Why? Why?' (*EP* 139). The implication, of course, as in *The White Hotel* or *Flying in to Love*, is that there is indeed 'something in the air', something in the public world of history which infects the private world of the individual. He begins to dream of a mass of bloated corpses, mostly Jews, tumbling out of a train, his sisters (both of whom were to be killed in concentration camps) among them; there is a smell of 'putrefying flesh' (*EP* 215), and, then, as the passengers are bundled naked into a bathhouse, a smell of gas. He dreams of a man named Stangl (the Treblinka commandant, though he does not know it) and one 'accused of killing millions of Jews' named Eckermann or Eichmann (*EP* 241). Then he dreams of a bright light followed by a cloud shaped like a mushroom, and a flattened city (*EP* 219). Freud doubled in this novel turns out to be precisely the kind of visionary neurotic Thomas had imagined him treating in *The White Hotel*.

Eating Pavlova ends with Freud dreaming one final dream. It is a version of a recurring dream Anna Freud really had in which her dead father appears, longing for her rather than the other way around, and which thereby demonstrates, she thought, how mourners project their own feelings onto the lost object.[5] The novel implies that Freud is the source of many projections, as a figure who has shaped contemporary consciousness as surely as the traumatic events of twentieth-century history. In his last dream Freud finds himself in his house, which is now cold, desolate, and empty. He sees Anna and is shocked at how small and frail she looks. He feels she has 'granted him a vision of how she will look in her last hours. Who will be left to mourn for Anna-Psyche herself when she descends into the shades?' (*EP* 274). He longs for her, the embodiment of psychoanalysis, the woman who did most to preserve his biographical memory, and the woman who knew most of all – except perhaps D. M. Thomas – the secret private Freud who existed beneath the public exterior.

After *Eating Pavlova* Thomas continued his interest in biography and its interconnection with the patterns of history, but took it in a more conventional direction, publishing in 1998 a lengthy biography of Solzhenitsyn, a work which has a good claim, along with its two predecessors, to be among Thomas's best. As the subtitle, *A Century in His Life*, suggests, the book tells the story of the turbulent Russian century, which of course to some extent represents the violence and trauma of the twentieth century as a whole, through the life of one individual, as *The White Hotel* does. As many reviewers pointed out, not all approvingly, Thomas invests the story with all the excitement and panoramic scope of a novel. But while its subject matter allows Thomas to exercise his capacity for vivid imagination, it also benefits from the constraints provided by having to stick to the known facts of one man's life. It reminds us, in other words, that Thomas has always produced his best material when working within the parameters of a pre-existing text, life, or historical event.

The point is reinforced by the novel that provided a diversion from his labour on *Solzhenitsyn*, which suffers from the lack of such imposed constraints. *Lady With a Laptop* (1996) was, perhaps significantly, published only in America and comes out of Thomas's own experiences leading writing classes on the Greek island of Skyros. It tells the story of a group of creative writing students and Simon Hopkins, their teacher, on the fictitious neighbouring island, Skagathos. The title points to a central intertext, Chekhov's 1899 story 'Lady With a Lap-Dog'. Yet the two have little in common beyond a general concern with love affairs: where Chekhov tells of a passionate illicit affair, the sexual relationships between

Thomas's characters are spiritless and empty. While this is actually in keeping with the novel's rhetoric about how the modern world of the laptop, the Internet, and corporate sponsorship, is extinguishing genuine artistic passion and spirituality, *Lady With a Laptop* struggles to rise above cliché in its depiction of character, Greece, or sex. Even the discussions of writing provide little real insight into Thomas's creative process, and the stories improvised by the various members of the group are pale imitations of some of those in *Russian Nights*. But its weaknesses do have the effect of reminding us what is strong in Thomas's work. What is subversive about Thomas is not his appropriation of controversial subject matter or having characters who say fuck all the time, but his peculiar strategies of incorporating intertexts in his fiction. Thomas is at his most powerful and original when bound to a precursor text; paradoxically, that is, he becomes most 'himself' as a writer when he is being someone else.

This conclusion is reinforced by Thomas's most recent novel, *Charlotte*, even though much of its story reduplicates the weaknesses of its predecessor. Miranda Stevenson, a Cornish-born academic from London visits the Caribbean island of Martinique to give a paper on Charlotte Brontë at an academic conference. She is registered for the conference under the name of 'Charlotte Brontë', after someone has mixed up her name and her subject on a form. This rather unlikely occurrence underlines the fact that the novel aims to present us with a version of the kind of woman Charlotte Brontë might have become if she had been born into a different, permissive age. There is no real sense, though, that Miranda is possessed by Brontë's spirit in the way in which previous Thomas characters (or the author himself) are inhabited by the spirit of Pushkin. Instead, the novel only really comes to life when Thomas *performs* the effects of authorial doubling rather than explores them through obvious ciphers like Miranda's mistaken identity.

After a manuscript purporting to be an alternative ending to *Jane Eyre* written by Brontë herself comes into her hands, Miranda writes a continuation of it to please her father, who collects Victoriana. The novel opens with this alternative version, and it is a characteristically faultless piece of mimicry.

It begins with the famous opening two lines of *Jane Eyre*'s last chapter – 'Reader, I married him. A quiet wedding we had: he and I, the parson and clerk, were alone present' – and then blends in Thomas's own impersonation with other sections of the original. Unlike the most famous rewriting of *Jane Eyre*, Jean Rhys's *Wide Sargasso Sea* (1966), Thomas's interest is in the second Mrs Rochester rather than the first. The novel's rationale is signalled by 'Jane's' complaint that 'It is well known that in novels – for example, the novels of Miss Austen – the pen falters just at the point where, perhaps, the most interesting narrative begins: *after* the wedding ceremony' (C 17–18). Thus Thomas takes issue with one of the most revealing ideological conventions of Victorian narrative, supremely exemplified in the last chapter of *Jane Eyre*: the idea that a character may become progressively enlightened or achieve redemption, but once their new identity is secured there will be no further change.

Thomas's Rochester is the most convincing creation in the novel, at once true to the original and also developed onto a plausible new level. Once his sight has begun to return, he becomes prone to unpredictable changes in mood, hinting at a disturbing undercurrent of violence and cruelty. This raises the question many ask when reading the last chapter of *Jane Eyre*, whether a man capable of imprisoning his first wife and confessing to having numerous 'mistresses' would entirely be able to shake off his Bluebeard qualities despite the physical punishment dealt out to him by Providence. As Rochester reveals to Jane, he is still (naturally enough) haunted by the events of the past. He eventually storms off after an argument, and is thrown from his horse and killed, suggesting that there is something unresolved in his conscious or unconscious mind.

Focusing on the married life of the Rochesters allows us to peer voyeuristically under the bedclothes of Victorian ideology and explore the world of what Steven Marcus famously called the 'other Victorians', that is, the hidden sexual dimension to Victorian society.[6] In this respect *Charlotte* resembles Thomas's previous excursion away from his usual fictional terrain into Victorian literature, *Swallow*'s 'scandalous amendment' of *King Solomon's Mines*. The comic effect of that piece of rewriting comes from Thomas's decision to preserve the nineteenth-century voice of the original and introduce a contemporary tone only sparingly: for example, ' "I say, you fellows," I sang out. "Won't you take some diamonds with you? I've filled my pockets." – "Oh! Bugger the diamonds!" said Sir Henry. "I hope that I may never see another"' (*Sw* 196). *Charlotte* is similarly restrained but less bawdy. Jane tells us that she refuses to 'draw a veil over the intimacies which transpire between a man and his wife' and gives a detailed account of her 'deflowering' on the marital bed (C 14–15). Gradually, though, incongruous contemporary discourse seeps in to the narrative, and the effect becomes more obviously parodic. *Jane Eyre*'s most famous line becomes echoed to the point of comedy: 'Reader, I was ignorant' (C 11), then 'Reader, I told him to piss off' (C 136). Later, with Maria Ashford (formerly Miss Temple of Lowood school), Jane discusses her experience of sex with Rochester and realizes that what she had taken to be sexual intercourse was actually no more than Rochester inserting his finger into her. Rochester, it transpires, is probably impotent. The exchange, while still more or less faithful to the literary conventions of Victorian dialogue, is funny, verging on the pornographic, but raises serious questions. Sex, of course, was a fact of life for Victorians; *Jane Eyre* was considered scandalous by many contemporary readers for its blatant sexual undercurrents. Though ashamed at her own sexual ignorance, Jane immediately decides to confront Rochester, as tactfully as she can, urging him to be open with her, stressing her 'understanding of the physical and mental difficulties he had faced after his heroic attempt to save the life of "that crazed woman"' (C 47). This is *Jane Eyre* with the post-Freudian sensibility of the modern woman. Rochester is not so modern, however, and disappears soon after, his manliness in tatters.

Thomas's take on *Jane Eyre* is not unprecedented. In his article 'Pornography and Obscenity', D. H. Lawrence discerned something 'pornographic' about the novel, regarding it as symptomatic of the way nineteenth-century bourgeois culture treated sexuality as something obscene rather than natural, with the result that sex became a kind of 'dirty little secret' which inspired its own kind of perverse sexual pleasure. This is why, he suggests, the novel can only acknowledge Rochester's passionate sexuality once he has been severely mutilated.[7] In Lawrence's terms, it is Brontë's *Jane Eyre* that is pornographic rather than D. M. Thomas's scandalous amendment, for Thomas brings the original's 'dirty little secret' out into the open, treating sex – as his Jane does – as a fundamental component of the human spirit.

The comparison between Thomas and the twentieth century's most provocative English novelist is quite appropriate, and not just because of their shared romantic temperament, their faith in the link between libidinal energy and creativity, or the influence of Lawrence on Thomas's first short story. Just as Lawrence was accused of producing pornography, when his work, in his view, was precisely the opposite, it is ironic that Thomas should so often be seen as a rather deceitful writer, when underlying his work is the desire to be honest about our libidinal investment in the traumatic events of our time and the aim to come clean about the collaborative essence of authorship.

Notes

CHAPTER 1. INTRODUCTION: DOUBTING THOMAS

1. Martin Amis, 'The D. M. Thomas Phenomenon', *Atlantic Monthly*, April 1983, 124–6.
2. The events are documented in news reports in, for example, the *Washington Post*, 27 January 1982 and 29 January 1982. Thomas himself gives a detailed account of the affair in his article 'On Literary Celebrity' and in *Memories and Hallucinations*. See also Lynn Felder, 'D. M. Thomas: The Plagiarism Controversy', in Richard Ziegfeld (ed.), *Dictionary of Literary Biography Yearbook 1982* (Detroit: Gale Research, 1983), 79–82.
3. Anatoli Kuznetsov, *Babi Yar*, trans. David Floyd (London: Sphere Books, 1970).
4. See the letters pages of the *Times Literary Supplement*, 26 March 1982 – 30 April 1982.
5. Acknowledgements page, *Penguin Modern Poets 11: D. M. Black, Peter Redgrove, D. M. Thomas* (Harmondsworth: Penguin, 1968).
6. Susanne Kappeler, *The Pornography of Representation* (Cambridge: Polity Press, 1986), 93.
7. Louise Doughty/D. M. Thomas, 'The Dirty Weekend', *Guardian Weekend*, 20 June 1992, 10–11.
8. Bryan Cheyette, review of *Pictures at an Exhibition*, *Times Literary Supplement*, 29 January 1993, 20.
9. Dealing with the Holocaust in art is almost by definition a controversial activity, as Sue Vice's introduction to *Holocaust Fiction* (London: Routledge, 2000) demonstrates.
10. D. M. Thomas, letter to the *Times Literary Supplement*, 30 April 1982, 487.
11. Dina Pronicheva herself is introduced towards the end of the Babi Yar section, as 'the only witness, the sole authority for what Lisa saw and felt' (*WH* 220–21). A number of critics have compared

Thomas's incorporation of *Babi Yar* with the original: e.g. D. A. Kendrick's original letter of accusation in the *Times Literary Supplement*, 26 March 1982; Patrick Swinden, 'D. M. Thomas and *The White Hotel*', *Critical Quarterly*, 24:4 (Winter 1982), 74–80 (79–80); Sue Vice, *Holocaust Fiction*, 40–44.

12. See the article in the *New York Times*, 'Author of "White Hotel" Criticized on New Work', 21 September 1982, 15; and original review: 'Pushkin Reunited', by Simon Karlinsky, *New York Times Book Review*, 26 September 1982, 11; see also Thomas's letter of defence: 'D. M. Thomas on his Pushkin', *New York Times Book Review*, 24 October 1982, 15. For the background to the allegations made by Carl R. Proffer, see Felder, 'The Plagiarism Controversy', 80.

13. In his second letter to the *Times Literary Supplement* Thomas points out that Grigson was probably only able to make the claim about his early poems because Thomas's own 'youthful' and 'unnecessarily scrupulous' acknowledgement alerted him to the original stories in the first place (*Times Literary Supplement*, 30 April 1982, 487).

14. Simon Karlinsky, 'Pushkin Reunited', *New York Times Book Review*, 26 September 1982, 11.

15. Linda Hutcheon, 'Literary Borrowing . . . and Stealing: Plagiarism, Sources, Influences, and Intertexts', *English Studies in Canada*, 12: 2 (1986), 229–39 (234).

16. Molly Nesbit, 'What was an Author', in Sean Burke (ed.), *Authorship: From Plato to the Postmodern: A Reader* (Edinburgh: Edinburgh University Press, 1995), 247–62 (248).

17. Roland Barthes, 'The Death of the Author', in Burke, *Authorship*, 125–30, Harold Bloom, *The Anxiety of Influence: A Theory of Poetry* (Oxford: Oxford University Press, 1973). Burke's book includes other important contributions to the debate on authorship, like Michel Foucault's 'What is an Author' (233–6).

18. This section hardly featured in the plagiarism controversy, supporting Hutcheon's claim that plagiarism has more to do with the kind of texts used than *how* they are used (Hutcheon, 'Literary Borrowing . . .', 230).

19. Sigmund Freud, 'The "Uncanny" ', *The Penguin Freud Library*, vol. 14, *Art and Literature* (Harmondsworth: Penguin, 1990), 335–76.

20. Peter Kemp, review of *Charlotte*, *Sunday Times*, 7 May 2000, 50.

21. Diane Johnson, review of *Ararat*, *New York Times Book Review*, 27 March 1983, 7.

22. Steven Connor, *Dumbstruck: A Cultural History of Ventriloquism* (Oxford: Oxford University Press, 2000).

23. Jeffrey Berman, 'Freud Revisited: *The White Hotel*', in *The Talking Cure: Literary Representations of Psychoanalysis* (New York and London: New York University Press, 1987), 270–94 (284).

24. Susan Sontag, 'The Pornographic Imagination', *A Susan Sontag Reader* (Harmondsworth: Penguin, 1982), 205–34 (214, 221–2).

CHAPTER 2. VOICES: *DREAMING IN BRONZE, BIRTHSTONE, THE FLUTE-PLAYER*

1. Biographical note, *Penguin Modern Poets 11: D. M. Black, Peter Redgrove, D. M. Thomas* (Harmondsworth, Penguin, 1968).

2. Anthony Clare, conversation with D. M. Thomas, *Listener*, 6 September 1990, 10–12 (10).

3. Clare, conversation with Thomas, 10.

4. D. M. Thomas, Preface to *Selected Poems* (New York: The Viking Press, 1983), p. vii.

5. All the poems discussed in this chapter can be found in *The Puberty Tree: New and Selected Poems* (Newcastle upon Tyne: Bloodaxe Books, 1992), except 'Botallack', originally in *Logan Stone* and also in *Selected Poems* (Harmondsworth and New York, 1983).

6. Thomas, Preface to *Selected Poems*, p. vii.

7. Clare, conversation with Thomas, 10. Imogen Edwards-Jones, conversation with D. M. Thomas, *The Times* 1F (21 February 1998), 14–15 (14).

8. Thomas, Preface to *Selected Poems*, p. viii.

9. William Borders Hereford, conversation with D. M. Thomas, *New York Times Book Review*, 24 March 1981, 7.

10. Edwin McDowell, conversation with D. M. Thomas, *New York Times*, 28 June 1981, 26.

11. Suzanne Cassidy, conversation with D. M. Thomas, *New York Times Book Review*, 8 July 1990, 3.

12. We could also regard as typically Celtic the interest in the demonic in the battle between Devil and St Michael in Thomas's only novel for children, *The Devil and the Floral Dance* (1978), which is set in Cornwall and which, incidentally, is a reminder that Thomas's excursion into prose for *Birthstone* was not his first.

13. Flora Rheta Schreiber, *Sybil* (Harmondsworth: Penguin, 1975).

14. Tzvetan Todorov, *The Fantastic: A Structural Approach to a Literary Genre*, trans. Richard Howard (London: Cornell University Press, 1975).

15. Thomas, Preface to *Selected Poems*, p. vii.

16. Edwards-Jones, conversation with Thomas, 14.
17. D. M. Thomas, Alexander *Solzhenitsyn: A Century in His Life* (1998; London: Abacus, 1999), p. xiv.
18. Sabine Durrant, conversation with D. M. Thomas, *Observer*, 6 September 1996, 17.
19. D. M. Thomas, Introduction to *Selected Poems of Anna Akhmatova* (Harmondsworth: Penguin, 1988), 11.
20. Thomas, Introduction to *Selected Poems of Anna Akhmatova*, 3.
21. D. M. Thomas, 'Variations On an Icon', review of Stephen Berg's *Akhmatova at the Black Gates, Washington Post Book World*, 2 August 1981, 5; Thomas, Introduction to *Anna Akhmatova*, 3.
22. Durrant, conversation with Thomas, 17.
23. Carl Gustav Jung et al., *Man and His Symbols* (London: Aldus Books, 1964), 177.

CHAPTER 3. THE ART OF SEDUCTION: *THE WHITE HOTEL*

1. Rare exceptions to the wholesale academic concern with *The White Hotel* are John Fletcher's essay on Thomas's 1987 novel *Summit* ('Thomas's Satire in Summit', *Studies in Contemporary Satire*, 18 (1991–2), 9–17), and Patrick Swinden's brief discussion of *Dreaming in Bronze* and *The Bronze Horseman*, in 'D. M. Thomas and *The White Hotel*', *Critical Quarterly*, 24:4 (Winter 1982), 74–80 (76).
2. Sigmund Freud, *Beyond the Pleasure Principle*, Pelican Freud Library, vol. 11 (Harmondsworth: Pelican, 1979).
3. See Jeffrey Berman's Appendix to his reading of the novel, 'Freud Revisited: *The White Hotel*', *The Talking Cure: Literary Representations of Psychoanalysis* (New York and London: New York University Press, 1987), 295–7. I have found his chronology of events in the novel most useful in writing my own account.
4. See, e.g., Peter Novick, *The Holocaust and Collective Memory* (London: Bloomsbury, 2000), and Norman Finkelstein, *The Holocaust Industry* (London and New York: Verso, 2000).
5. Sue Vice, *Holocaust Fiction* (London: Routledge, 2000), 38.
6. Rowland Wymer, 'Freud, Jung and the "Myth" of Psychoanalysis in *The White Hotel*', *Mosaic: A Journal for the Interdisciplinary Study of Literature*, 22:1 (1989), 55–69.
7. Many readings of the novel argue that Freud systematically destroys Lisa's individuality less violently but just as brutally as the Final Solution: e.g. Linda Hutcheon, 'Subject In/Of/To History and His Story', in *A Poetics of Postmodernism: History,*

Theory, Fiction (London: Routledge, 1988), 158–77; Laura E. Tanner, 'Sweet Pain and Charred Bodies: Figuring Violence in *The White Hotel*', *boundary* 2, 18:2 (1991), 130–49; Patricia Waugh, *Harvest of the Sixties: English Literature and its Background 1960–1990* (Oxford: Oxford University Press, 1995), 74; Swinden, 'D. M. Thomas and *The White Hotel*'.

8. Swinden, 'D. M. Thomas and *The White Hotel*', 76.
9. Berman, 'Freud Revisited', 270.
10. The device is central to the category of fiction Linda Hutcheon calls 'historiographic metafiction'. Hutcheon's and Alison Lee's readings of *The White Hotel* consider this aspect of the novel alongside other contemporary examples like Julian Barnes's *Flaubert's Parrot*: see Hutcheon, 'Subject In/Of/To History and His Story', 158–77, and Alison Lee, *Realism and Power: Postmodern British Fiction* (London: Routledge, 1990), 94–8.
11. 'Elisabeth von R.', in Sigmund Freud and Joseph Breuer, *Studies on Hysteria*, Pelican Freud Library, vol. 3 (Harmondsworth: Pelican, 1974), 202–58.
12. In a letter to Hereward Carrington, 24 July 1921; see Berman, 'Freud Revisited', 338 n. 26.
13. Baudrillard's critique of psychoanalysis is developed over three books: *Seduction* (New York: St Martin's Press, 1990), *Simulacra and Simulation* (Ann Arbor: The University of Michigan Press, 1994), and *Symbolic Exchange and Death* (London: Sage, 1993). See also John Forrester, *The Seductions of Psychoanalysis: Freud, Lacan, Derrida* (Cambridge: Cambridge University Press, 1994).
14. Hutcheon argues that *The White Hotel* 'is in some ways a profoundly anti-humanistic novel that problematizes the same issues as poststructuralist theory' ('Subject In/Of/To History and His Story', 166). In questioning this I am not denying there is a close similarity between the novel's effects and the interests of poststructuralist theorists, but I do see such a reading as an example of the 'seductions' of literary criticism, where the critic finds his or her own interests mirrored in the object of attention. To read *The White Hotel* purely in terms of how it foregrounds questions of discourse and textuality is too easy. The novel may well show how humanist/rationalist discourse is 'defeated' by liberating, subversive postmodernist/poststructuralist discourse, but it also suggests that Lisa is destroyed by naked power, thus reminding us that history is determined by the eruption of the traumatic unsymbolizable real as much as by the conflict of discourses.

15. Carl Gustav Jung, 'Conscious, Unconscious and Individuation', in Anthony Storr (ed.) *Selected Writings* (London: Fontana, 1998), 216.

16. Jung, 'Confrontation with the Unconscious', in *Selected Writings*, 77. Jung argued elsewhere that 'the gigantic catastrophes that threaten us today are not elemental happenings of a physical or biological order, but psychic events' ('The Development of Personality', in *Selected Writings*, 200).

17. Wymer, 'Freud, Jung and the "Myth" of Psychoanalysis in *The White Hotel*', 58–9.

18. See Lisa Appignanesi and John Forrester, *Freud's Women* (London: Virago, 1993), 204–26.

19. D. M. Thomas, review of Aldo Carotenuto's *A Secret Symmetry: Sabina Spielrein Between Jung and Freud, New York Review of Books*, 13 May 1982, 3–6. Thomas belatedly wrote Sabina Spielrein into *The White Hotel* in his second novel which 'doubles' Freud, *Eating Pavlova*. There Freud mentions that Spielrein once encountered another patient of his while at the Kiev opera.

20. Marguerite Alexander, 'Breakdown', *Flights from Realism: Strategies in Postmodernist British and American Fiction* (London: Edward Arnold, 1990), 103.

21. Sigmund Freud, 'The Unconscious', Penguin Freud Library, vol. 11 (Harmondsworth: Penguin, 1991).

22. See Lee, *Realism and Power*, 94–8.

23. This response is encapsulated in a comment from one of the enthusiastic American reviews which helped make the book so popular: 'I quickly came to feel that I had found that book, that mythical book, that would explain us to ourselves' (Leslie Epstein, review of *The White Hotel, New York Times Book Review*, 15 March 1981, 1).

24. D. M. Thomas, letter to the *Times Literary Supplement*, 30 April 1982, 487.

CHAPTER 4. ACTING OUT: THE *RUSSIAN NIGHTS* QUINTET

1. D. M. Thomas, Introduction to *The Bronze Horseman* (Harmondsworth: Penguin, 1982), 25.

2. Suzanne Cassidy, conversation with D. M. Thomas, *New York Times Book Review*, 8 July 1990, 3.

3. Thomas, Introduction to *The Bronze Horseman*, 12.

4. Ibid, 21.
5. E.g. in his biography of Solzhenitsyn: *Alexander Solzhenitsyn: A Century in His Life* (1998; London: Abacus, 1999), 289–90.
6. Cassidy, conversation with Thomas, 3.
7. Roland Barthes, *S/Z*, trans. by Richard Miller (New York: Hill and Wang, 1974), 90.
8. The poem can be found in *The Puberty Tree*, 133.
9. Imogen Edwards-Jones, conversation with D. M. Thomas, *The Times*, 1F (21 February 1998), 14–15 (14).
10. Thomas, review of *Operation Shylock: A Confession* by Philip Roth, *New York Times Book Review*, 7 March 1993.
11. See Anthony Clare, conversation with D. M. Thomas, *Listener*, 6 September 1990, 10–12 (10).
12. Sigmund Freud, *Totem and Taboo*, Penguin Freud Library, vol. 13, (Harmondsworth: Penguin, 1990), 133.

CHAPTER 5. DREAMTIME: *FLYING IN TO LOVE* AND *PICTURES AT AN EXHIBITION*

1. Linda Hutcheon, *A Poetics of Postmodernism: History, Theory, Fiction* (London: Routledge, 1988).
2. Suzanne Cassidy, conversation with D. M. Thomas, *New York Times Book Review*, 8 July 1990, 3.
3. Robert Jay Lifton, *The Nazi Doctors: Medical Killing and the Psychology of Genocide* (New York: Basic Books, 1986).
4. The Schubert quartet of the same name is also referred to, however. 'Pictures at an Exhibition' is not one of Munch's works but the title of the famous piano suite composed by Russian composer Mussorgsky in 1874 to accompany a series of paintings by Victor Hartmann, just as Thomas's *Pictures at an Exhibition* accompanies Munch's.
5. Munch tended obsessively to do more than one version of his major works and *Pictures at an Exhibition* does not state which version of *Death and the Maiden* is referred to. The most appropriate example, though, seems to be the drypoint version of 1894, which I go on to discuss.
6. Bryan Cheyette, review of *Pictures at an Exhibition*, *Times Literary Supplement*, 29 January 1993, 20.
7. Hannah Arendt, *Eichmann in Jerusalem: A Report on the Banality of Evil* (Harmondsworth: Penguin, 1994).
8. Daniel R. Schwarz, *Imagining the Holocaust* (New York: St Martin's Press, 1999).

CHAPTER 6. DOUBLING THOMAS: *EATING PAVLOVA* AND *CHARLOTTE*

1. In *The Times*, 1994, reproduced on the back of the paperback edition.
2. E.g., Freud explains that the genesis of his essay on the uncanny was seeing doubles of his sons (*EP* 177). We can surmise that the occasion when Freud is visited by three guests, Lou Andreas-Salomé, Isaac Newton and Charles Darwin (*EP* 20), is a reference to 28 June 1938, when he was visited by a representative of the Royal Society and asked to add his signature to a list including both illustrious scientists (Peter Gay, *Freud: A Life for Our Time* (London: Macmillan, 1989), 681). His admission that 'I am in favour of an infinitely free sexual life, though I have myself not followed my own precept . . .' (*EP* 138) echoes a well-known statement from one of his letters to J. J. Putnam in 1918: 'I stand for an infinitely freer sexual life, although I myself have made very little use of such freedom' (Ernst L. Freud, trans. Tania and James Stern (eds.), *Letters of Sigmund Freud 1873–1839* (London: The Hogarth Press, 1970)). The central premise of *Eating Pavlova* is given plausibility by the publication, two years before, of *The Diary of Sigmund Freud 1929–1939: A Record of the Final Decade*, ed. and trans. by Michael Molnar (London: Hogarth/Freud Museum, 1992).
3. Sigmund Freud, *The Interpretation of Dreams*, Pelican Freud Library, vol. 4 (Harmondsworth: Pelican, 1976), 209.
4. John Farrell has argued something similar about the real Freud in *Freud's Paranoid Quest* (New York: New York University Press, 1996).
5. The epigraph to the novel is an account of this dream by Anna Freud. The source of the quotation is unspecified, though it is an abridged version of a passage from a draft of a paper Anna Freud was working on in 1948 called 'About Losing and Being Lost'. For more details, see Lisa Appignanesi and John Forrester, *Freud's Women* (London: Virago, 1993), 302.
6. Steven Marcus, *The Other Victorians: A Study of Sexuality and Pornography in Mid-Nineteenth-Century England* (London: Weidenfeld & Nicolson, 1967).
7. D. H. Lawrence, 'Pornography and Obscenity', in *À Propos of Lady Chatterley's Lover* (Harmondsworth: Penguin, 1961), 60–84.

Select Bibliography

WORKS BY D. M. THOMAS

Novels

The Flute-Player (London: Victor Gollancz, 1979).
Birthstone (London: Victor Gollancz, 1980).
The White Hotel (London: Victor Gollancz, 1981).
Ararat (London: Victor Gollancz, 1983).
Swallow (London: Victor Gollancz, 1984).
Sphinx (London: Victor Gollancz, 1986).
Summit (London: Victor Gollancz, 1987).
Lying Together (London: Victor Gollancz, 1990).
Flying in to Love (London: Bloomsbury, 1992).
Pictures at an Exhibition (London: Bloomsbury, 1993).
Eating Pavlova (London: Bloomsbury, 1994).
Lady With a Laptop (New York: Carroll and Graf, 1998).
Charlotte (London: Duckworth, 2000).

Poetry

Personal and Possessive (London: Outposts, 1964).
Penguin Modern Poets 11: D. M. Black, Peter Redgrove, D. M. Thomas (Harmondsworth: Penguin, 1968).
Two Voices (London: Cape Goliard, 1968).
The Lover's Horoscope: Kinetic Poem (Laramie, Wyoming: Purple Sage, 1970).
Logan Stone (London: Cape Goliard, 1971).
The Shaft (Gillingham, Kent: Arc, 1973).
Lilith-Prints (Cardiff: Second Aeon, 1974).
Symphony in Moscow (Richmond, Surrey: Keepsake Press, 1974).
Love and Other Deaths (London: Elek Books, 1975).
The Rock (Knotting, Bedfordshire: Sceptre Press, 1975).

Orpheus in Hell (Knotting, Bedfordshire: Sceptre Press, 1977).
The Honeymoon Voyage (London: Secker and Warburg, 1978).
Protest: A Poem after a Medieval Poem by Frik (private printing, 1980).
Dreaming in Bronze (London: Secker and Warburg, 1981).
News from the Front, with Sylvia Kantaris (Todmorden, Lancashire: Arc, 1983).
Selected Poems (Harmondsworth and New York: Viking, 1983).
The Puberty Tree: New and Selected Poems (Newcastle: Bloodaxe, 1992).

Translations

Anna Akhmatova, *Requiem and Poem Without a Hero* (London: Elek Books, 1976).
Anna Akhmatova, *Way of All the Earth* (London: Secker and Warburg, 1979).
Yevgeny Yevtushenko, *Invisible Threads* (New York: Macmillan, 1981).
Alexander Pushkin, *The Bronze Horseman and Other Poems* (London: Secker and Warburg, and Harmondsworth: Penguin, 1982).
Yevgeny Yevtushenko, *A Dove in Santiago* (London: Secker and Warburg, 1982).
Alexander Pushkin, *Boris Godunov* (Leamington Spa: Sixth Chamber Press, 1985).
Anna Akhmatova, *You Will Hear Thunder: Poems* (London: Secker and Warburg, 1985); reprinted as *Selected Poems* (Harmondsworth: Penguin, 1988).

Memoir

Memories and Hallucinations (London: Victor Gollancz, 1988).

Biography

Alexander Solzhenitsyn: A Century in His Life (London: Little, Brown, 1998).

Other

The Granite Kingdom: Poems of Cornwall (editor) (Truro, Cornwall: Barton, 1970).
Poetry in Crosslight (editor) (London: Longman, 1975).
Songs from the Earth: Selected Poems of John Harris, Cornish Miner, 1820–84 (editor) (Padstow, Cornwall: Lodenek Press, 1977).
The Devil and the Floral Dance (children's novel) (London: Robson Books, 1978).

'Freud and *The White Hotel*', *British Medical Journal*, 287 (24–31 December 1983), 1957–60.

INTERVIEWS

Gonzalez, Rosa, 'Art and the Unseen Pattern in the Universe: An Interview with D. M. Thomas', *Barcelona English Language and Literature Studies*, 3 (1989) 63–70.

Lewis, Stephen, 'D. M. Thomas', *Art out of Agony: The Holocaust Theme in Literature, Sculpture and Film* (Toronto: Canadian Broadcasting Corporation, 1984), 71–88.

Wingrove, David, 'Different Voices', *London Magazine*, February 1982, 27–43.

CRITICISM

Alexander, Marguerite, 'Breakdown', *Flights from Realism: Strategies in Postmodernist British and American Fiction* (London: Edward Arnold, 1990), 97–103.

Amis, Martin, 'The D. M. Thomas Phenomenon', *Atlantic Monthly*, April 1983, 124–6.

Barnsley, John H., '*The White Hotel*', *The Antioch Review*, 40:4 (1982), 448–60.

Bartkowski, Frances, and Catherine Stearns, 'The Lost Icon in *The White Hotel*', *Journal of the History of Sexuality*, 1:2 (1990), 283–95.

Bayley, John, 'The Greatness of Akhmatova: *Requiem* and *Poem Without a Hero* translated by D. M. Thomas', *Selected Essays* (Cambridge: Cambridge University Press, 1984), 138–48.

——'Looking in on Pushkin', *Selected Essays* (Cambridge: Cambridge University Press, 1984), 103–15.

Berman, Jeffrey, *The Talking Cure: Literary Representations of Psychoanalysis* (New York and London: New York University Press, 1987), 270–94.

Bradbury, Malcolm, 'The White Mountain (D. M. Thomas)', *No, Not Bloomsbury* (London: André Deutsch and Arena, 1987), 349–51.

Brown, Lady Falls, '*The White Hotel*: D. M. Thomas's Considerable Debt to Anatoli Kuznetsov and *Babi Yar*', *South Central Review*, 2:2 (1985), 60–79.

Cowart, David, 'Being and Seeming: *The White Hotel*', *Novel*, 19:3 (1986), 216–31.

Cross, Richard K., 'The Soul is a Far Country: D. M. Thomas and *The White Hotel*', *Journal of Modern Literature*, 18:1 (1992), 19–47.

Ellery, Chris, 'Oracle and Womb: Delphic Myth in D. M. Thomas', *The White Hotel*', *Notes on Contemporary Literature*, 19:3 (1989) 3–4.

Felder, Lynn, 'D. M. Thomas: The Plagiarism Controversy', in Richard Ziegfeld (ed.), *Dictionary of Literary Biography Yearbook 1982* (Detroit: Gale Research, 1983), 79–82.

Fletcher, John, 'Thomas's Satire in Summit', *Studies in Contemporary Satire*, 18 (1991), 217.

Foster, John Burt, 'Magic Realism in *The White Hotel*: Compensatory Vision and the Transformation of Classic Realism', *Southern Humanities Review*, 20:3 (1986), 205–19. Revised version: 'Magical Realism, Compensatory Vision, and Felt History: Classical Realism Transformed in *The White Hotel*', in Lois Parkinson Zamora and Wendy B. Faris (ed.), *Magical Realism: Theory, History, Community* (Durham, NC: Duke University Press, 1995), 267–83.

Gabbard, Krin, '*The White Hotel* and the Traditions of Ring Composition', *Comparative Literature Studies*, 27:3 (1990), 230–48.

George, Diana, 'Teaching the Nightmare World of *The White Hotel*', *Proteus: A Journal of Ideas*, 6:1 (1989), 57–60.

Granofsky, Ronald, 'Holocaust as Symbol in *Riddley Walker* and *The White Hotel*', *Modern Language Studies*, 16:3 (1986), 172–82.

Higdon, David Leon, 'Solomon's Fair Shulamite in D. M. Thomas' *The White Hotel*', *Journal of Modern Literature*, 19:2 (1995), 328–33.

Hughes, Mary Joe, 'Revelations in *The White Hotel*', *Critique*, 27:1 (1985), 37–50.

Hutcheon, Linda, 'Subject in/of/to History and His Story', *Diacritics*, 16:1 (1986), 78–91. Reprinted in: Linda Hutcheon, *A Poetics of Postmodernism: History, Theory, Fiction* (London, Routledge, 1988), 158–77.

Kappeler, Susanne, 'Art and Pornography', *The Pornography of Representation* (Cambridge: Polity Press, 1986), 82–100.

Kinder, Marsha, 'The Spirit of *The White Hotel*', 4:2–3 (1981), 143–70.

Ledbetter, Mark, 'The Body Human and the Body Community: Getting the Story Write/Right in D. M. Thomas's *The White Hotel*', *Victims and the Postmodern Narrative, or Doing Violence to the Body: An Ethic of Reading and Writing* (London: Macmillan, 1996), 72–87.

Lee, Alison, *Realism and Power: Postmodern British Fiction* (London: Routledge, 1990), 94–8.

Leighton, Lauren G., 'Translation and Plagiarism: Pushkin and D. M. Thomas', *Slavic and East European Journal*, 38:1 (1994), 69–83.

Lougy, Robert E., 'The Wolf-Man, Freud, and D. M. Thomas: Intertextuality, Interpretation and Narration in *The White Hotel*', *Modern Language Studies*, 21:3 (1991), 91–106.

McClintick, Michael, 'Modern Man in Search of His Art: Jung's Theory of Man's Creative Nature', *Willamette Journal of the Liberal Arts*, 4:2 (1989), 13–31.

MacInnes, John, 'The Case of Anna G.: *The White Hotel* and Acts of Understanding', *Soundings: An Interdisciplinary Journal*, 77:3–4 (1994), 253–69.

Malcuzynski, M.-Pierrette, 'Polyphonic Theory and Contemporary Literary Practice', *Studies in Twentieth Century Literature*, 9:1 (1984), 75–87.

Michael, Magali Cornier, 'Materiality Versus Abstraction in D. M. Thomas's *The White Hotel*', *Critique*, 43:1 (2001), 63–84.

Newman, Robert D., 'Another White Hotel', *Notes on Contemporary Literature*, 21:4 (1991), 3–4.

——'D. M. Thomas' *The White Hotel*: Mirrors, Triangles, and Sublime Repression', *Modern Fiction Studies*, 35:2 (Summer 1989), 193–209.

Ozsvath, Zsuzsanna, and Martha Satz, 'The Audacity of Expressing the Inexpressible: The Relation Between Moral and Aesthetic Considerations in Holocaust Literature', *Judaism*, 34:2 (1985), 197–210.

Phillips, K. J., 'The Phalaris Syndrome: Alain Robbe-Grillet vs. D. M. Thomas', in Katherine Anne Ackley (ed.), *Women and Violence in Literature: An Essay Collection* (New York: Garland, 1990), 175–205.

Punter, David, 'The Politics of Fear', *The Hidden Script: Writing and the Unconscious* (London: Routledge, 1985), 113–28.

Robertson, Mary F., 'Hystery, Herstory and History: "Imagining the Real" in Thomas's *The White Hotel*', *Contemporary Literature*, 25:4 (1984), 452–77.

Sauerberg, Lars Ole, 'Fact-Flirting Fiction: Historiographical Potential or Involuntary Parody?', *European Journal of English Studies*, 3:2 (1999), 190–205.

——'When the Soul Takes Wing: D. M. Thomas's *The White Hotel*', *Critique*, 31:1 (1989), 3–10.

Sayre, Henry M., 'The Avant-Garde and Experimental Writing', in Emory Elliott, Martha Banta and Houston A. Baker (eds.) *The Columbia Literary History of the United States* (New York and Guilford: Columbia University Press, 1988), 1178–99.

Scherr, Rebecca, 'The Uses of Memory and the Abuses of Fiction: Sexuality in Holocaust Fiction and Memoir', *Other Voices: A Journal of Critical Thought*, 2:1 (2000) (no pagination).

Siegelman, Ellen Y., '*The White Hotel*: Visions and Revisions of the Psyche', *Literature and Psychology*, 33:1 (1987), 69–76.

Stovel, Nora Foster, 'Tatiana's Letter, A Literary Legacy: From Pushkin's 'Eugene Onegin' to D. M. Thomas's *White Hotel*', *International Fiction Review*, 25:1/2 (1998), 1–11.

Swinden, Patrick, 'D. M. Thomas and *The White Hotel'*, *Critical Quarterly*, 24:4 (Winter 1982), 74–80.

Tanner, Laura E., 'Sweet Pain and Charred Bodies: Figuring Violence in *The White Hotel'*, *boundary* 2, 18:2 (1991), 130–49.

Todd, Richard, 'Convention and Innovation in British Fiction, 1981–1984: The Contemporaneity of Magic Realism', in Theo D'haen and Helmut Lethen (eds.) *Convention and Innovation in Literature* (Amsterdam and Philadelphia, PA: John Benjamins, 1989), 361–88.

Vice, Sue, 'Documentary Fiction: D. M. Thomas, *The White Hotel'*, in *Holocaust Fiction* (London: Routledge, 2000), 38–66.

Waugh, Patricia, 'Keeping Our Metaphysics Warm', *The Harvest of the Sixties: English Literature and its Background 1960–1990* (Oxford: Oxford University Press, 1995), 71–5.

Weber, Jim, '*The White Hotel*: Freud, Medusa, and the Missing Goddess', *Notes on Contemporary Literature*, 21:1 (1991), 10–11.

Wirth-Nesher, Hana, 'The Ethics of Narration in D. M. Thomas's *The White Hotel'*, *The Journal of Narrative Technique*, 15:1 (1985), 15–28.

Wren, James A., 'Thomas's *The White Hotel'*, *Explicator*, 54:2 (1996), 123–6.

Wymer, Rowland, 'Freud, Jung and the "Myth" of Psychoanalysis in *The White Hotel'*, *Mosaic: A Journal for the Interdisciplinary Study of Literature*, 22:1 (1989), 55–69.

Young, James E., 'Holocaust Documentary Fiction: The Novelist as Eyewitness', in Berel Lang and Aron Appelfeld (eds.), *Writing and the Holocaust* (New York: Holmes & Meier, 1988), 301–11.

Zhang, Benzi, 'The Chinese Box in D. M. Thomas's *The White Hotel'*, *International Fiction Review*, 20:1 (1993), 54–7.

OTHER WORKS CITED

Appignanesi, Lisa, and John Forrester, *Freud's Women* (London: Virago, 1993).

Arendt, Hannah, *Eichmann in Jerusalem: A Report on the Banality of Evil* (Harmondsworth: Penguin, 1994).

Barthes, Roland, 'The Death of the Author', in Sean Burke (ed.), *Authorship: From Plato to the Postmodern: A Reader* (Edinburgh: Edinburgh University Press, 1995), 125–30.

——*S/Z*, trans. Richard Miller (New York: Hill and Wang, 1975).

Baudrillard, Jean, *Seduction* (New York: St Martin's Press, 1990).

——*Simulacra and Simulation* (Ann Arbor: The University of Michigan Press, 1994).

——*Symbolic Exchange and Death* (London: Sage, 1993).

Bloom, Harold, *The Anxiety of Influence: A Theory of Poetry* (Oxford: Oxford University Press, 1973).

Connor, Steven, *Dumbstruck: A Cultural History of Ventriloquism* (Oxford: Oxford University Press, 2000).

Farrell, John, *Freud's Paranoid Quest* (New York: New York University Press, 1996).

Finkelstein, Norman, *The Holocaust Industry* (London and New York: Verso, 2000).

Forrester, John, *The Seductions of Psychoanalysis: Freud, Lacan, Derrida* (Cambridge: Cambridge University Press, 1994).

Freud, Ernst L. (ed.), *Letters of Sigmund Freud 1873–1839*, trans. Tania and James Stern (London: The Hogarth Press, 1970).

Freud, Sigmund, *Beyond the Pleasure Principle*, Pelican Freud Library, vol. 11 (Harmondsworth: Pelican, 1979).

——*The Diary of Sigmund Freud 1929–1939: A Record of the Final Decade*, ed. and trans. Michael Molnar (London: Hogarth/Freud Museum, 1992).

——*The Interpretation of Dreams*, Pelican Freud Library, vol. 4 (Harmondsworth: Pelican, 1976).

——*Totem and Taboo*, Penguin Freud Library, vol. 13 (Harmondsworth: Penguin, 1990).

——'The Unconscious', Penguin Freud Library, vol. 11 (Harmondsworth: Penguin, 1991).

——and Joseph Breuer, *Studies on Hysteria*, Pelican Freud Library, vol. 3 (Harmondsworth: Pelican, 1974).

Gay, Peter, *Freud: A Life for Our Time* (London: Macmillan, 1989).

Hutcheon, Linda, 'Literary Borrowing . . . and Stealing: Plagiarism, Sources, Influences, and Intertexts', *English Studies in Canada*, 12:2 (June 1986), 229–39.

——*A Poetics of Postmodernism: History, Theory, Fiction* (London: Routledge, 1988).

Jung, Carl Gustav, et al., *Man and His Symbols* (London: Aldus Books, 1964).

Jung, Carl Gustav (ed.) *Selected Writings*, ed. Anthony Storr (London: Fontana, 1998)

Kuznetsov, Anatoli, *Babi Yar*, trans. David Floyd (London: Sphere Books, 1970).

Lawrence, D. H., 'Pornography and Obscenity', in *À Propos of Lady Chatterley's Lover* (Harmondsworth: Penguin, 1961), 60–84.

Lifton, Robert Jay, *The Nazi Doctors: Medical Killing and the Psychology of Genocide* (New York: Basic Books, 1986).

Marcus, Steven, *The Other Victorians: A Study of Sexuality and Pornography in Mid-Nineteenth-Century England* (London: Weidenfeld & Nicolson, 1967).

Nesbit, Molly, 'What was an Author', in Sean Burke (ed.), *Authorship: From Plato to the Postmodern: A Reader* (Edinburgh: Edinburgh University Press, 1995), 247–62.

Novick, Peter, *The Holocaust and Collective Memory* (London: Bloomsbury, 2000).

Schreiber, Flora Rheta, *Sybil* (Harmondsworth: Penguin, 1975).

Schwarz, Daniel R., *Imagining the Holocaust* (New York: St Martin's Press, 1999).

Sontag, Susan, 'The Pornographic Imagination', in *A Susan Sontag Reader* (Harmondsworth: Penguin, 1982), 205–34.

Todorov, Tzvetan, *The Fantastic: A Structural Approach to a Literary Genre*, trans. Richard Howard (London: Cornell University Press, 1975).

Index

Printed and bound by CPI Group (UK) Ltd, Croydon, CR0 4YY

13/04/2025

14656597-0005